101 Nine Patch Quilts

by Marti Michell

Bobbie Matela, Managing Editor
Carol Wilson Mansfield, Art Director
Linda Causee, Editorial Director
Christina Wilson, Assistant Editor
Illustrations and Editorial Assistance: Patti Lilik Bachelder
Editorial Assistance: Jenny Lynn Price
Graphic Solutions Inc-Chgo, Book Design

For a full-color catalog including books on
quilting, write to:
American School of Needlework®
Consumer Division
1455 Linda Vista Drive
San Marcos, CA 92069
or visit us at:
http://www.asnpub.com

Contents

About the Author

Marti Michell loves teaching people to make quilts that look complicated, but really aren't. That's why she loved compiling 101 Nine Patch Quilts, her 17th book for ASN Publishing. She has been involved in quiltmaking since 1969 and "in the business" since 1972, but is still fascinated with how much excitement can be created with the simplest blocks.

If you have quilted a long time, you may remember Yours Truly, Inc., founded in 1972 by Marti and her husband, Richard and owned by them until it was sold in 1985. Since 1995, they have become known for From Marti Michell acrylic templates for rotary cutting. Whether Marti is participating in quilting as a teacher, quilter, author, publisher, manufacturer, designer, consultant, judge or quilt collector, her enthusiasm for and love of quilting is always evident. In 1991, she received the first Quilt Industry Lifetime Achievement Award.

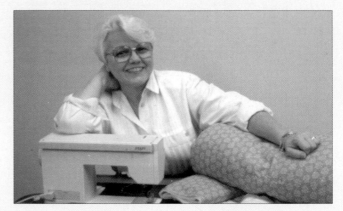

Marti was born and raised in Iowa and received a B.S. in Textiles and Clothing and Home Economics Journalism from Iowa State University. She and Richard are at home in Atlanta, Georgia. Their two children are gone, but the two cats remain.

The Challenge

When I was writing *Quilting for People Who STILL Don't Have Time to Quilt*, the enlarged revised version of *Quilting for People Who Don't Have Time to Quilt*, my publisher, Rita Weiss, and I reluctantly decided to reduce the number of Nine Patch quilts in the book. We also agreed that the quilts we had eliminated would make a nice little book limited to Nine Patch designs.

Sometime later, Rita mentioned the series of books ASN was doing featuring 101 designs. With a little sarcasm, I said, "I guess that means I have to come up with 101 Nine Patch variations." Well, after many years of

friendship, I understood the look on Rita's face. Accompanied by her immediate question, "Could you really do that?" I knew my next book was going to be a collection of 101 Nine Patch Quilts.

First, I searched the many books I have written and collected the Nine Patch variations. After that I scoured books of antique quilts for additional combinations. Then, with that base, Patti Bachelder, a quilter and a whiz with the Macintosh computer and Illustrator program, began making more variations for me—hundreds of times faster by computer than the old graph paper and colored pencil way.

101 Nine Patch quilts would not have been compiled without her effort and imagination.

For more information about strip cutting and strip techniques, refer to either *Quilting for People Who STILL Don't Have Time to Quilt*, ASN book #4183, published in 1998, or *Quilting for People Who Don't Have Time to Quilt*, ASN book #4111, published in 1988.

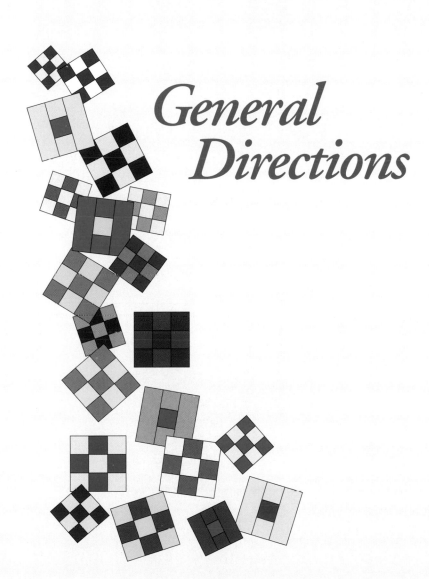

General Directions

Nine Patch quilts might be called the backbone of American quiltmaking. Many of us envision little girls in pioneer America practicing their needlework skills by stitching Nine Patch blocks by candlelight! At the same time, a quick look at reference books will show that the popularity of the Nine Patch has never diminished.

There are few blocks that are so simple and so powerful at the same time. Nine Patches can be made into great quilts or used as zippy accents. This may be a record for the largest number of Nine Patch quilt designs collected between the covers of one book, but the point is to stress the versatility of the Nine Patch. In addition, as you look through other quilt books, you'll recognize more easily the Nine Patch repeat and be able to adapt techniques from this book.

Anatomy of the Nine Patch

Most often people think of the Nine Patch as five squares of one fabric and four of a contrasting fabric set together in a checkerboard pattern, **Diagram A.** The squares are also typically thought of as the same size. One of the first things you will see is that there can be many other combinations of color and size, but the construction technique will still be the same.

Diagram A

The Nine Patch is perfect for beginners.

What could be easier? The Nine Patch is made with squares and straight line sewing. In the most basic combination, it is simply a checkerboard of alternating colors or values.

The Nine Patch is Perfect for Strip Techniques.

With everything the Nine Patch already had in its favor, the arrival of the rotary cutter really enhanced the simplicity of construction of this block. It was no longer necessary to cut nine individual squares for every block. The rotary cutter, ruler and protective mat resulted in the popularity and growth of strip techniques.

In a Nutshell

Using strip techniques in quiltmaking means that you learn to recognize the repeat patterns of squares and strips— then cut and sew strips together, cut again, and rearrange to complete sewing. Another way to say this is that you will learn to think and see in patchwork grids.

Strip techniques allow you to enjoy making quilts for people to enjoy using! You will be making quilts that can be finished in hours, not months or years. The techniques include rotary cutting, cutting multiple layers, machine piecing and machine quilting. (See more about strip techniques on the following pages.)

I avoid using the words "easy" or "fast" or "quick" because too many people turn up their noses, assuming those words mean big pieces, sloppy workmanship, low standards. No-No-No! Strip techniques introduced here for the Nine Patch are easier, faster and more accurate than what could be called traditional techniques.

The Nine Patch is perfect for scrap quilts.

No matter how clever we get using carefully planned Nine Patch subunits to make new and larger geometric designs, the classic scrap Nine Patch quilts continue to be sentimental favorites of quilters everywhere. Using scraps does not prevent using strip techniques.

The Nine Patch Can Be Any Size!

One of the wonderful things about strip techniques is that any size strip you can cut will make a different size Nine Patch. For practical purposes, it makes more sense to cut easy-to-measure strip widths—1 inch, 1 1/2 inches, 2 inches, etc. that make 3-, 4 1/2- and 6-inch finished blocks than to cut strips for 5-inch blocks. Typically, the larger the finished project, the larger the finished Nine Patch should be and the larger the first strip will be. Block sizes that are easily divisible by three are among some of the most popular sizes in quilting, so that makes combining the Nine Patch with other blocks fairly easy, too.

When you look at the quilt layouts in this book, you will see that finished measurements are given for the layout shown. The calculation is usually based on the smallest square in the quilt finishing to either 1 inch or 2.5 centimeters. That doesn't mean we expect you to make the quilts this size. It is simply a starting point. Because the designs in this book are based on a 1-inch grid unit, you can multiply the size given by a new grid unit size to see what size the quilt would be if the smallest square finished to that size.

Don't feel restricted to the easy measurements. In reality, with the availability of good acrylic rulers and rotary cutters, even increments of 1/8 inch are quite easy to measure and cut. A 1/8-inch difference in a finished square isn't very obvious, but can make a big difference in the total number of patchwork units needed. You can see an example on pages 80 and 81, where I chose to make 1-inch squares for the new quilt instead of 7/8-inch squares that were used in the antique quilt. By so doing, I eliminated both a vertical and horizontal row of Nine Patch units.

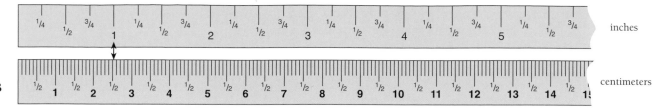

Diagram B

The Nine Patch translates easily to metric.

Strip techniques and, therefore, Nine Patch blocks are just as wonderful if you cut and sew in metric as if you work in imperial measurements (inches). When you look at the quilt layouts in this book, you will see that finished measurements are given for each layout shown. The calculation is usually based on the smallest square in the quilt finishing to either 1 inch or 2.5 centimeters. Because the design is on a grid, there are no pattern pieces: the finished size of the block is determined by the width of the first strip.

Most other times when measurements are discussed in inches, you will need to substitute the metric measurement. Use the ruler above to find the closest easy-to-use conversion, **Diagram B**.

There Are No Pattern Pieces in This Book!

You do not need pattern pieces or templates if the quilt design can be drawn on a grid. Instead, you will learn to use the grid to represent measurements and eliminate pattern pieces. Perhaps the most empowering feature of quilts drawn on grids is that you decide what size pieces to work with. You are not confined to fixed pattern piece sizes and only one finished block size. The size of the first strip you cut determines the scale and finished size of the project. For example, in **Diagram C**, there is a grid 4 squares wide by 5 squares high. If each square represents 1 inch (cut size 1 1/2 inches), the shape would be 4 inches by 5 inches; if each square represents 2 inches (cut size 2 1/2 inches), the shape would be 8 inches by 10 inches; if each represents 10 inches

(cut size 10 1/2 inches), the shape would be 40 inches by 50 inches; and if each square represents 3 cm (cut size 4.2 cm), the finished shape would be 12 cm by 15 cm, etc.

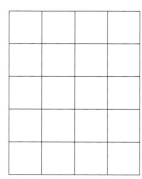

Diagram C

The most frequently used shapes in patchwork are strips, squares and right triangles. Squares, of course, are just strips cut so their length is the same as their width. Right triangles can be cut from squares. All of them can be drawn on a grid such as graph paper. The blocks in the first section of quilts in this book deal exclusively with strips and squares. In the second section of quilts, triangles are only used as a device for completing rows in the diagonal set quilts. In the third section, other techniques and shapes are included.

Repetition in the order of the fabrics is the crucial ingredient for efficient strip techniques. When the size and shape of a piece repeats consistently and frequently, as in most Nine Patch quilts, strip techniques can be used to the maximum. For every square in a repeating grid pattern, you will cut a strip as wide as the finished size of the square plus 1/2 inch (two 1/4-inch seam allowances). The strip will be as long as you want or is convenient. My routine length is 27 inches cut on the lengthwise grain, but I will occasionally use 45 inches cut on the crosswise grain.

The Sew-Before-You-Cut Theory

In a Nutshell

How you actually sew the pieces together unlocks the secrets of the "Quilting for People Who Don't Have Time to Quilt" techniques. Erase completely from your mind the idea of making a quilt piece by little piece. Remember, everything that you can Sew-Before-You-Cut is more accurate, faster and easier.

In *Quilting for People Who* Still *Don't Have Time to Quilt*, I used a "nutshell" technique. That means I gave the highlights or minimum information in a boxed area, and followed with explanations and details. In this book, I'll do the same.

Sew-Before-You-Cut is one way of describing strip-piecing techniques which are the backbone of the Nine Patch. You will quickly learn to appreciate these techniques by actually using them. It is hard to do them justice in words. In this case, a few minutes of action is worth a thousand words.

Sew-Before-You-Cut is almost revolutionary. It's different from anything you were taught in sewing class. The old patchwork ways of cutting and sewing one piece at a time incorporated very little thought. You do need to think ahead and organize a little for the Sew-Before-You-Cut methods to be most effective. The first thing is to analyze the pattern and develop a plan for what pieces you can Sew-Before-You-Cut. In the quilt layouts that begin on page 25, the accompanying illustrations are designed to help you develop a plan.

This book focuses on the Nine Patch. See either the *Quilting for People* series or *Quilting for People Who STILL Don't Have Time to Quilt* for more complete information on strip techniques, and for many other quilt designs that benefit from using strip techniques.

Tools for Accurate Cutting

Some of my quilt-making friends love the quilting most, some prefer the piecing process, but I don't know anyone who says, "I can't wait to get home and cut!" Yet accurate cutting is the first crucial step in accurate patchwork.

One of the reasons the techniques in this book are so effective is the use of the rotary cutter, introduced in 1979. It is used with a protective mat and an acrylic ruler to speed you through the cutting process and get you to the fun part. Let's face it, cutting can be pretty tedious, especially if you are looking at a quilt and design and seeing nearly 1000 squares to cut. Doesn't it sound better to say 100 strips? Or by cutting multiple layers, 25 cuts? Even more important than speed is accuracy. The rotary cutting system is quicker and more precise than cutting with scissors, and has revolutionized the ease of cutting most shapes, especially strips!

The reason I stress this so much is that I ignored the rotary cutter for several years after I first saw it. After all, I reasoned, I had good scissors and I could use them well. Surely this advanced pizza cutter was just a gadget - right? Wrong! Today it is much more likely that you will have been introduced to the rotary cutter than when my first books appeared, but just in case you haven't, now is the time.

There are several rotary cutters on the market. They came in two sizes for years, 28 mm and 45 mm, but recently a very large cutter, 60 mm, has been introduced. Some people feel more comfortable starting with the smallest cutter. If you want to keep your initial investment down, it is also less expensive. Because I am almost always doing multiple layer cutting, I prefer either of the larger cutters.

People say to me, "How can you use that to cut fabric and not cut your table?" You can't! That's where the protective mat comes in. You must use the cutter on the mat if you don't want your table to look like the bottom of a used pizza pan!

Don't try a homemade substitute for a protective mat. Leftover linoleum doesn't work. Old stacks of newspaper won't work. The mat designed for the job is self-healing and does not dull the blade like other surfaces might. There are many sizes and as you might suspect, the larger the mat, the more expensive.

Back to the actual cutting process. To be effective in cutting strips with a rotary cutter, you need a strong straight edge. There are many different acrylic rulers on the market, 5 inches or 6 inches wide and 24 inches long. The grid on the ruler surface is extremely helpful in assuring accuracy. Most of the rulers also have angles and other special features printed on them.

Tip *Rotary Cutter Tips & Techniques*

- The blades are very sharp. All of the brands currently available have guards. Make sure the guard is in place when the cutter is not in use. This protects both you and the blade. If you drop the cutter or accidentally cut across a pin, the blade often becomes nicked. Then instead of cutting the fabric where the blade is nicked, it perforates the fabric. The blades are replaceable, but the need can be minimized if you will just keep the guard in place.

- A fresh blade will cut six to 12 layers of fabric easily with very little pressure. Bearing down too hard is not necessary and can do irreparable damage to the protective mat. It's harder to accurately fold and stack 12 layers of fabric than to cut them. For that reason, I generally cut four to eight layers even though the cutter could cut more.

- When cutting, the blade side, not the guard side, goes immediately next to the acrylic ruler.

- Cut away from you, not toward your body.

- To get straight strips, it is imperative that the ruler be perpendicular to the fold on folded fabrics and/or parallel to the selvage. The preliminary cut is usually to trim off the selvage (cutting strips on the lengthwise grain) or to straighten a store cut edge (cutting strips on the crosswise grain), either of which creates one side of the first strip. Cutting the second side of the strip requires changing hands, going to the other side of the mat, or turning the mat. My favorite method is to cut the first strip left-handed—not as hard as it sounds if you have a good ruler—and the rest of the strips right-handed, which is my favored hand; then I don't have to change table sides or turn the fabric or mat.

- Specific guidelines for using the rotary cutting system to cut sewn strip sets are included in The Second Cut, page 11.

Seam Allowances

In a Nutshell

The recommended seam allowance is 1/4 inch, using 10-12 stitches per inch. It is generally not necessary to back-stitch at the ends of the seams as you will stitch across most ends almost immediately.

If you are new to quilting and patchwork, you may not have entered the world of the 1/4-inch seam allowance yet. After using 5/8-inch seam allowances in dressmaking, the first 1/4-inch seam will look impossibly thin. Try to remember that many of the 5/8-inch seam allowances survive being trimmed smaller than 1/4 inch, turned inside out and poked.

On some sewing machines the outside edge of the presser foot is exactly 1/4 inch from the center of the needle hole. An easy way to check is to put a tape measure under your presser foot. Put any inch mark at the needle. Put the presser foot down, **Diagram D**. If it's 1/4 inch, you're lucky. If it isn't, there are several other ways to create a 1/4-inch seam guide. For now, when you are just sewing strips, a guide on the throat plate or a piece of tape can be lined up to show where to run the edge of the fabric. Check with your sewing machine dealer to see if there is a 1/4-inch presser foot attachment available for your machine. Many newer machines have a variable needle position that may create a perfect 1/4-inch seam allowance.

Diagram D

There's More to Perfect Patchwork than a 1/4-inch Seam Allowance
In the final analysis, it's the size of the finished patchwork piece that is really important, not the size of the seam allowance. The seam allowance is there to keep the sewing threads from ripping out and to allow you to make adjustments if necessary. The object is to have a perfect 1-inch square in the finished patchwork, for example, not to have a perfect 1/4-inch seam allowance. Too often people get all hung up on sewing exactly 1/4 inch from the cut edge. This is fine when it works, and when you have both a perfect finished piece and a perfect seam allowance you can feel very smug, but the most important thing is the perfect size finished patchwork.

With strip techniques, consistency counts most.

It is also true that in this book that emphasizes strip techniques, it is consistency that counts. Cutting, sewing and pressing perfectly result in mathematically correct measurements. What happens if the edge of your presser foot makes a seam just a little larger or smaller than 1/4 inch? The size of your finished unit is just a little smaller or larger, and is called your one-and-only unique measurement. As long as all of the seams are the same, it is not a crisis. When a unit block or quilt interior is just a little larger or smaller than intended, adjustments to the finished quilt size can be made easily by slightly changing the size of borders or sashing strips.

With strip techniques, I emphasize the cut size, and cutting accuracy. Then with consistent sewing, the finished sizes are accurate shapes. This is not true with complicated, multi-shape and angular pieces or curved seams. With those shapes, you must know exactly what size seam allowance is on the pattern or included in the template and make sure you are really stitching the correct seam allowance. Since you do need to know how to make a 1/4-inch seam for some quilts, life will be easier if you just learn how now.

Pressing

In a Nutshell

Pressing is not optional!

It is smart to make your iron one of your best friends as you embark on patchwork. My preference is a steam iron. When pressing seams in patchwork, both seam allowances go in the same direction, not open as in dressmaking. When in doubt, press them toward the darker fabric.

When I am pressing a set of strips, I usually put the strips across the ironing board instead of end to end. With the seam allowances right side up, I hold onto the fabric with my left hand and put the iron down on the other edge of the strips. With the weight of the iron holding the right hand side of the fabric, I put just a little tension on the left side. That causes the seam allowances to stand up, and with the steam iron, I can press them down flat. Keep the strips straight; don't press curves into your strips.

Pressing strip sets is easiest when all seams go in the same direction, but many times the instructions for Nine Patch blocks are to press toward the darker fabric. That often means that seams need to go in opposite directions on the same strip set. Sometimes you can press from each side in toward the center. Sometimes you have to hold the strip at the end and work your way down the middle. You do what you have to do to get it right! Time spent pressing carefully is time well spent.

With the philosophy that once is not enough, I then turn the strips over and press from the right side of the fabric. The object is to eliminate any tiny folds I might have pressed into the seam. Tiny $1/32$-inch folds don't seem like much until you multiply that times two for each seam, and times four or five seams for a block, and times ten or 12 for the number of blocks. I admit to being a fanatic about perfect pressing!

Directional Pressing

Directional pressing is especially conducive to the ease and accuracy of making Nine Patch blocks. The side effect of directional pressing is what I call automatic pinning. The seam allowances butt against each other when the units are positioned for sewing, and often eliminate the need to pin.

Some of the Fence Rail/Nine Patch combination quilts, such as Quilt 41, Sticks 'n Stones, can be more easily made if you press all the seams in one direction, regardless of color.

Typically, you will press between each step. Some people like to set up a pressing area right beside the sewing machine and stay seated while pressing. I don't mind getting up to press. I usually have sewn so many strips or sets together while at the machine that getting up to press gives me a chance to stretch.

Short Cut Pressing

Short cut pressing is not recommended for strip sets, but may be useful when joining the sub-units of a quilt. Sometimes finger pressing can postpone pressing for one step. Using a combination of your fingers and the presser foot tension to hold the seam allowance in place, you can usually stitch across the most recent seam adequately. I never go more than one step without a full pressing. You have to decide which is more important to you: perfect, flat seams or saving a few minutes on every quilt you make for the rest of your life. Everything is a trade-off.

The "Second Cut"

This is really your first opportunity to put the Sew-Before-You-Cut theories to work. Now that your first strips are cut, pieced and pressed, you make the second cut that forms the second dimension of the patchwork piece, **Diagram E**. The width of the strips formed the first dimension. Again, go to the rotary cutter and mat, and perhaps switch to a shorter acrylic ruler. True up one end of the strip set. Then measure from that end for the next cut. When truing up or making the second cut across sewn strip sets, line up the ruler with horizontal seams. It is important that the second cut be both perpendicular to the seams and be parallel to the end of the strip set.

Sew-Before-You-Cut means you are working with larger pieces, and it is easier to be accurate with larger pieces. Stated another way, an error of $1/16$-inch is a much greater problem on a 2-inch piece than an 8-inch piece.

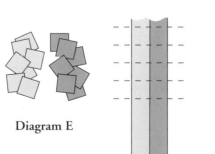

Diagram E

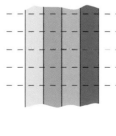

Chain Piecing

Strip piecing is the process of sewing two strips together, **Diagram E**. Chain piecing means continuously feeding the pieces to be joined under the presser foot without cutting the thread, **Diagram F**. Even though the strips are actually chain pieced, chain piecing more commonly refers to the piecing done after the second cut. As you place the same combination of pieces in position, one after the other, it is easy to see any obvious visual differences. These are visual warnings. Likewise, it is easy to make a consistent slight change to correct a problem from the previous step. This is something that you will have to look at and analyze as you sew; each quilt is different and I could write words forever, but experience is the real teacher.

Correcting Any Differences

Diagram F

Measure several units to determine if they match the MCM or are your O&O. If you have several different O&O's for the same unit, adjustments are necessary! After measuring several units, you will know whether a slight adjustment or a huge one is required.

If the sub-units or unit blocks are slightly varying sizes, there are several possible solutions. Double-check your pressing: you may have pressed folds into the seams, which can be corrected with re-pressing. Look at the seam allowances: are they consistent? Check the strips themselves: were they cut evenly? It may be necessary to take out a few seams to make adjustments. The wide

Tip *How to Calculate the Number of Strips to Cut for each Fabric*

The number of strips to cut is, of course, determined by several things. Let's figure the yardage required when strips are cut on the crosswise grain. We will convert to cutting strips on the lengthwise grain later.

a. _____ What width is the strip in question?

b. _____ What will be the size of the second cut across the strip or strip set (increment length for the segments)?

c. _____ Divide 42" (106.7cm) by the answer to b to determine how many segments will be in one strip and drop any partial number.

d. _____ Count or calculate how many segments are needed in the quilt.

e. _____ Divide the answer to d by the answer to c to find the number of strips required. Round up to the next number.

f. _____ Multiply the answer to e by the answer to a to find the minimum yardage requirement. Refer to the yardage conversion chart below.

g. _____ Do you think you will want to use this fabric in the borders? If yes, calculate the approximate amount and amend the total yardage.

acrylic rulers with grids printed on them can become very useful to check the accuracy of sizes, confirm that seams are perpendicular and finally to use with the rotary cutter to accurately trim excess edges.

If the variance is large, you will need to carefully measure each unit and sort by size. If you made extras, they will come in handy now; you can set aside the most out-of-whack units to be used later for accessories. If you didn't make extras and there are only one or two very large or very small units, you may prefer to make replacements rather than compromise all of the others.

Sometimes straightening a seam is necessary because there is an equal error in both pieces of fabric. As long as the new seam allowance is wider than the old one, straightening simply requires a new seam, no ripping. The old stitching can stay in the seam allowance.

Some Tips on Ripping

If you must rip, the gentlest way is the best. On one side of the seam, cut about every sixth stitch. A little experimentation will let you know if you can get by with clipping every seventh or eighth stitch. Then turn the fabric over and pull the thread on the other side. When you cut at the right frequency, the thread just pops out as you pull. Go back to the first side and brush away the clipped threads.

Another ripping technique is to pull one thread, gathering the fabric on the seam, until it breaks. Then go to the other side of the fabric and pull the opposite thread until it breaks. Proceed back and forth until the seam is removed. This is faster and neater, but it is harder on the fabric and more likely to cause distortion.

Determining Yardage for Strip Cutting

The number and length of strips is determined by many factors, not the least of which is the size of the quilt.

Yardage Conversion Chart

1/8 yd	.125	4 1/2"
1/4 yd	.25	9"
3/8 yd	.375	13 1/2"
1/2 yd	.5	18"
5/8 yd	.625	22 1/2"
3/4 yd	.75	27"
7/8 yd	.875	31 1/2"
1 yd	1.0	36"

Let's practice by figuring the yardage required when strips are cut on the crosswise grain. We'll look at Quilt 20, Argyle, page 37. The desired finished size of the smallest square will be 1 1/2 inches. It makes sense to figure the easiest fabric first—that would be the dark tan alternate square.

Calculating the Dark Tan Fabric

a. __5"__ What width is the strip in question? This strip needs to be the same size as the Nine Patch, which is the total of three finished strips of 1 1/2 inches plus two 1/4-inch seam allowances.

b. __5"__ What will be the size of the second cut across the strip or strip set (increment length for the segments)? Since we want a square this should be the same dimension as the width.

c. __8__ Divide 42" (106.7 cm) by the answer to b to determine how many segments are in one strip and drop any partial number. 8.25 is rounded down to 8 inches.

d. __90__ How many segments of strip set are needed in the quilt? 18 Double Nine Patch blocks times 5 tan squares each = 90.

e. __12__ Divide the answer to d by the answer to c to find the number of strips required. Round up to the next number. 90 divided by 8 equals 11¼ strips.

f. _1¾ yds._ Multiply the answer to e by the answer to a to find the minimum yardage requirement. Refer to the yardage conversion chart below. 12 strips times 5 inches = 60 inches. 1 yard is 36 inches. 60 inches minus 36 inches is 24 inches. 1 yard and 24 inches is closest to 1¾ yard.

g. _1¾ yds._ Do you think you will want to use this fabric in the borders? If yes, calculate the approximate amount and add to f. Let's say the borders are 6½ inches wide and we need about 360 inches of length. Cutting on the crosswise grain, 42 goes into 360 more than 8 times. So 9 times 6.5 = 58.5 inches. Close enough to the 60 inches we got in f. to just add another 1¾ yards.

h. _4 yds. Total._ When I add f & g, I get 3½ yards, but that leaves very little extra in either section. What if I want a wider border or I forgot to add the seam allowance for the border? I'm going to be more comfortable with buying 4 yards.

Cutting Strips on the Lengthwise Grain

Since I prefer my strips to be cut on the lengthwise grain (see Learning About Grainline, page 18), there is another step to consider. You generally need the same amount of fabric whether you cut strips on the lengthwise or crosswise grain. Occasionally, the calculations allow so little tolerance or extra fabric that if the second cut segments are unusually long they can't be cut efficiently on the lengthwise grain from the same amount of fabric. It rarely happens on pieces over ¾ yard.

Obviously since this is a 4 yard purchase, I can not only cut my strips on the lengthwise grain, I will want to make sure that I reserve a section where I can cut the borders on the lengthwise grain, (see **Diagram G**).

use

save for borders

Diagram G

This is not to recommend cutting a strip 4 yards long. After allowing for the borders, cut across the remainder of the fabric to get a usable length. I really like strips about ¾ yard (70 cm) long, but anything from 18-inch to 45-inch long strips can work.

Sometimes people ask why I calculate yardage based on crosswise measurements when I adamantly recommend cutting strips on the lengthwise grain. They forget the length of the fabric is what we are calculating. It is the variable, while the crosswise measurement (42 usable inches) is practically a universal consistent number.

Calculating the Teal Fabric

The second easiest fabric to figure for the Argyle quilt would be the teal.

a. __2"__ What width is the strip in question? 1½ inches finished plus two quarter inch seam allowances.

b. __2"__ What will be the size of the second cut across the strip or strip set (increment length for the segments)?

c. __21__ Divide 42 inches (106.7 cm) by the answer to b and drop any partial number.

d. __289__ How many segments of strip set are needed? 17 in each of 17 Double Nine Patch blocks.

e. __14__ Divide the answer to d by the answer to c to find the number of strips required. Round up to the next number.

f. _1 yd._ Multiply the answer to e by the answer to a to find the minimum yardage requirement. Refer to the yardage conversion chart below. 28 inches would round up to ⅞ yard, but I'm going for a full yard.

Estimating the Red Fabric

What about the other fabrics in the Argyle quilt? Well a quick calculation tells me that I need 496 segments of red the same size as the 289 pieces of teal. Rounding up, that is about 1½ times as much red as teal. I am really happy doing a short-cut calculation and buying a yard and a half of red.

Estimating and Calculating the Ecru Fabric

The last fabric to figure is the light ecru. It is used in both Double Nine Patch blocks and is two different sizes. I'm still in a short-cut mood. Again, it doesn't take long to multiply the number of small squares in each of the Double Nine Patch blocks by the number of blocks and add those two totals for a whopping 628 small squares. (Aren't you glad you won't cut them individually?) That is a little more than twice as many teal squares. We rounded up and bought a yard of teal, it seems that 2¼ yards of light ecru will be adequate for the squares in the Nine Patch units. But more light ecru fabric is needed for the large alternate squares in the Double Nine Patch units. They are the same size as the dark tan fabric we figured first, so all of the figures would be the same up to step d of that fabric. Let's start from there.

d. __68__ How many segments of strip set are needed in the quilt? 17 Double Nine Patch blocks times 4 ecru squares each.

e. __9__ Divide the answer to d by the answer to c to find the number of strips required. Round up to the next number. 68 divided by 8 equals 8½ strips.

f. 1¼ yds Multiply the answer to e by the answer to a to find the minimum yardage requirement. Refer to the yardage conversion chart, page 12. Nine strips times 5 inches = 45 inches. One yard is 36 inches. 45 inches minus 36 inches is 9 inches. 1¼ yard.

g. no Do you think you will want to use this fabric in the borders?

h. 3½ yds This is the total from the estimated amount above and this calculation.

That would be a total of 10 yards for the quilt top. That fits with my rough estimates in How Much Fabric Do I Need? page 17.

Estimating Yardage for Nine Patch Blocks
Maybe you just want to estimate yardage for the Nine Patch portion of a quilt like Atlanta Commons on pages 100 to 101. You can use this handy chart to estimate the number of quarter yards (approximately 25 cm) of fabric you will need.

Determine the number and size of squares needed. Move down the chart to the appropriate size square and then across the chart to see the yield from one fat quarter yard or ½ yard of fabric.

If the quantity you need is greater than either column, divide your number of squares by the number of squares from one fat quarter. Round up to the next full number. That is the minimum number of quarter yards to buy.

Example: 176, 2½" squares

176 ÷ 42 = 4.2 rounded up to 5 fat quarters or 1¼ yards

What Size Is a Quilt?

How much fabric you need to buy is really a function of what size quilt you are making. With each diagram we have calculated the size the quilt would be if the smallest square is 1 inch finished, and likewise if it is 2.5 cm. Of course, you always have the option to make the quilt larger or smaller, depending upon your needs. Change size by changing strip width or by changing the borders. When you make quilts just because you want to, they can be any size.

Size is only crucial when you are making a quilt for a specific bed. Even then personal choices enter into size. Do you want it to hang to the floor or just skim a dust ruffle? Do you like a deep pillow tuck with huge pillows or will your quilt go under pillows? The best way to know what size you want is to put a large bed sheet on the chosen bed so that it hangs down and tucks and covers as you like. Then measure the sheet from edge to edge. Add 2 inches to 4 inches in both directions to compensate for the amount of shrinkage that occurs with the quilting. That is your optimum size. Be aware that as you get into planning quilts for specific sizes, compromises often have to be made. A 12-inch unit block, for example, doesn't always fit the perfect number of times in both directions, leaving an equal amount for borders all around. With the Nine Patch, the obvious solution is to change the strip width and make exactly the size block you need for your quilt.

Wallhanging is the term generally used in this book to define a quilt that was not made for a bed. Many of those quilts could also be used as throws or decorative table covers just as easily; the choice is yours. Quilts can be any size. Mini and miniature are descriptive words I like to use for quilts smaller than 24 inches in either dimension. "Mini" just means distinctly smaller, as in mini skirt; while "miniature" really denotes a copy made to a smaller scale.

Equivalent Number of Squares from One Fat Quarter
(18" x 22 ½", 45.7 cm x 57.1 cm)

Size of Square	Cut Strip Width	Approximate Qty from 1 Fat Qtr*	½ yd (45 cm)	Cut Width (Metric)
1"	1½"	168	336	4 cm
1¼"	1¾"	120	240	4.5 cm
1½"	2"	90	180	5 cm
1¾"	2¼"	72	144	5.75 cm
2"	2½"	56	112	6.5 cm
2¼"	2¾"	42	84	7 cm
2 ½"	3"	42	84	7.5 cm
2¾"	3¼"	30	60	8.25 cm
3"	3½"	30	60	9 cm
3¼"	3¾"	20	40	9.5 cm
3½"	4"	20	40	10 cm

*A fat quarter is 18" x 22½". It is a more useable size than a 9" x 45" quarter-yard.
For calculating purposes, 18" x 21" (45.7 cm x 53.3 cm) was used because widths on fabrics can vary and therefore the available amount of fabric will vary.

When measuring the bed isn't an option, I use these quilt size guidelines. Except for the crib size, they were developed by adding 9 inches for a pillow tuck at one narrow end and a 13-inch drop to the other three sides of the most common standard mattress sizes in the United States.

Crib -

small, 30 inches x 45 inches; or 76.2 cm x 114.3 cm

large, 40 inches x 60 inches; or 101.6 cm x 152.4 cm.

Twin -

65 inches x 97 inches; or 165.1 cm x 246.4 cm

Double -

80 inches x 97 inches; or 203.2 cm x 246.4 cm

Queen -

86 inches x 102 inches; or 218.4 cm x 259.1 cm

Queen/Double -

84 inches x 100 inches; or 213.4 cm x 254 cm

King -

104 inches x 102 inches; or 264.2 cm x 259.1 cm

If you have a different size mattress, make your own similar diagram to get a feeling for the percentage and positioning of the design that shows on the surface of a bed.

65" x 97"
165.1 cm x 246.4 cm

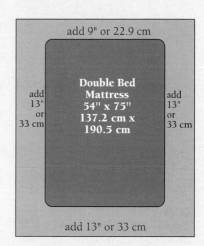

80" x 97"
203.2 cm x 246.4 cm

86" x 102"
218.4 cm x 259.1 cm

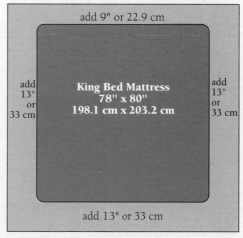

104" x 102"
264.2 cm x 259.1 cm

Patchwork Basics

One of the hard things about writing books is the need or desire to repeat some of the same basic information. Yet, the concern is that if you own more than one of my books, you'll consider it repetitious. Even though this is not meant to be a complete "How to Quilt" book, rather an inspiration for all of the things you can do with the Nine Patch, I feel the need to cover a few basic ideas.

Fabric Selection

In a Nutshell

There are a few things I feel duty-bound to say about fabric selection and fabric preparation. The nutshell synopsis is this: I like to use 100% cotton fabrics that have been tested for shrinkage and fading. I cut my strips on the lengthwise grain. I like to think of my fabric selections as spirited, pretty, surprising or even off-the-wall (if that is the statement I want to make), but not dull or boring, which is different from comfortable or safe.

Cotton helps prevent distortion. Cotton holds a press or crease, which is especially important for appliqué. Cotton seems to reduce the risk of batting "bearding" or fiber migration. Cotton is more comfortable. Cotton is easier to hand quilt. All of this is not to say you must use 100% cotton. It's just to say you should understand the possible problems if you don't. Generally, the more similar the fabrics are in weight and feel, the less the problem. A fabulous assortment of prints and solids are available today in 100% cotton. If you are a beginner, it will be easier if you start by limiting yourself to 100% cotton.

Look for Variety

In a Nutshell

You are making quilts to express yourself, to satisfy your own creative urges, to make a statement or tell a joke. Select the fabric accordingly. Variety is not only the spice of life, it will make your quilts more interesting. A nutshell approach to fabric selection is to look for variety in the fabrics you are combining in a quilt. Not just variety in the colors, but in the scale of the prints, the type of prints, the density, etc. Random designs maximize the ease of strip techniques. Directional designs require much more thought, but the result may make it worthwhile. Last, but perhaps most important, remember that the fabrics selected do more to set the mood of the quilt than the quilt design.

Here are a few fabric selection tips.

1. It is easy to be boring. Most beginners tend to be very "matchy-uppy." Often the result is that when you step back a few feet from the finished item, the fabrics just blend together.

2. Being happy with your quilt is most important. Use the pictures as a guide, but don't hesitate to change the colors, border sizes and arrangements. Your fabrics will look different from those photographed. Remember, the real key is that you are happy, because it is your quilt.

3. The fabrics set the mood of the quilt. Fabric does much more to set the mood of the quilt than the quilt pattern chosen. Even though most of the Nine Patch quilts feature crisp lines, the selection of feminine looking fabrics will make a very feminine quilt.

4. The appearance of texture in fabrics should not be overlooked or under-rated. In general, printed solids (defined as monochromatic or low contrast small prints) just add texture.

I often use them instead of solids. From a distance, the quilt has a softer more muted look. Close up, a texture print does not demand fancy quilting. Conversely, solids demand to be quilted, and so can look very empty without lots of hand quilting. In fact, if you are planning lots of fancy hand quilting, think solid-colored fabric.

5. Larger prints are not a no-no! When you cut a large print into smaller pieces, the images are often completely lost, only the colors and some random shapes remain.

6. Stripes and other directional designs need special consideration. The strong directional effect of stripes demands that special attention must be given to their cutting and placement in patchwork. When well done, the illusions of motion and action created with stripes can be breathtaking. Real-life motifs, such as trees, people or buildings whose tops all point in the same direction, and other single-direction designs are very time-consuming to plan into a quilt. Nearly all one-way designs should be avoided in quilts that are designed on point.

7. Random designs maximize the efficiency of strip techniques. Look carefully at your fabric choice. Directional fabrics can sneak in almost unnoticed. If in doubt, lay a small piece of fabric on top of and at right angles to the larger piece of fabric. If you would object to having some pieces going both ways in a quilt, it is directional. A fabric can be directional in either one way or two ways. Stripes are an example of a two-way directional fabric. Vertical stripes are meant to run up and down: sideways is obviously the wrong direction, but for many stripes, upside down has the same appearance as right side up. An animal print with all the animals oriented in the same direction, however, is a one-way directional: there is only one way to place the fabric so that the print looks like it was intended to look.

Conversely, fabrics with random patterns maximize the ease of strip techniques, require no special planning and will not look different when viewed from different angles. Refer to Fenced-in Chickens, page 52.

8. Consider room color. If you are making a quilt for a particular room, that color scheme will influence your thoughts, but should not rule them. I always like to encourage quilters to feel free about the fabrics they use and let the choices be right for the quilt, not the room. Funny thing, usually what is good for the quilt is good for the room.

9. Stand back before you buy or cut fabrics selected for a quilt. We all tend to select fabrics at no more than an arm's length. But we rarely look at the finished quilt from that distance. Instead, it is viewed from "across the room." The fabrics can look very different then.

10. Be prepared to change your mind. Even the most experienced quilter can be surprised at the way selected fabrics are going to look when they are cut and sewn together.

How Much Fabric to Buy?

In a Nutshell

My policy has always been to buy as much as I can afford.

In some ways, saying I buy as much as I can afford is a joke. In reality, once you start making lots of quilts, you will have a real appreciation for working from a stockpile of fabric. As quiltmakers, our fabric supply is our palette. If we don't have a fabric in a certain color, we can't use that color.

If you get very serious about quiltmaking, you will probably start collecting fabric. Perhaps you are thinking about quilting because you have already collected a considerable quantity of fabric. Being an experienced speculative fabric buyer myself, let me pass on my standard purchasing amounts. Use these standards or create your own, but you will discover that having established

standard purchasing lengths prevents embarrassing indecisiveness at the cutting table. If you have ever heard yourself saying, "I'd like 1/2 yard, please....No, make it 7/8....No, 5/8 should do....Oh, cut a yard and a half....No, just a yard. Yes, I'm sure," you know what I mean.

The least amount I ever ask store personnel to cut is 27 inches (3/4 yard, or approximately 70 cm). That's not an arbitrary amount. I like to use many different fabrics in most of my large quilts and I also make quite a few small quilts. Using fabric in those ways, 3/4 yard is almost always enough. Since almost everything I do starts with a strip, and because I cut my strips on the lengthwise grain whenever possible, 27 inches has also turned into my standard strip length. (Refer to Strip Piecing and Grainline, page 19.) Of course, if you plan to make full size quilts with only two or three fabrics, you need to buy more.

If I'm crazy about a fabric and/or think I might want to use it as a border on a large quilt, I buy 3 1/2 yards. That is the most I would need to cut a king-size border with mitered corners on the lengthwise grain. I can still cut small patchwork pieces down one side and leave a long wide piece of fabric along the other selvage for borders (see **Diagram G**, page 13). Even though I rarely make a final choice of border fabrics until I have completed the quilt interior, that doesn't prohibit me from buying some border fabrics speculatively.

Fat quarters (18 inches x 22 1/2 inches), available in many stores, are a nice way to purchase a small quantity of a wide variety of prints and still be able to cut a meaningful strip on the lengthwise grain (18 inches).

How Much Fabric Do I Need?

Now, if the question "How much fabric to buy?" is rephrased to "How much fabric do I need?" the answer is a little different. Just as there is no single fabric yardage requirement to

make a dress, there is not one answer for how much fabric it takes to make a quilt. Here are some rules of thumb. The backing alone for a queen/double requires 7 1/2 yards. So, if you add fabric for seams and some latitude in cutting, I say you need a minimum of 10 yards for the surface of a not-too-complicated queen/double quilt top. Following the same line of thought, you need a minimum of 12 1/2 yards for a king or 6 1/2 yards for a twin.

Many Nine Patch quilts are wonderful in a scrappy look, However, many demand consistency of fabric to make a design clearly visible. Because we are showing ideas and you have to make a decision about the finished size that you want to make, we can't give yardage requirements. See pages 12 to 14 for detailed information on calculating fabric. Almost everyone agrees having extra is better than agonizing over running out. More and more I find I use my extra yardage for pieced backs for quilts or to make pillow cases. I put them on top of the quilt propped against the bed, then I don't have to fight the pillow tuck battle.

Two important things about fabric purchases are:

1. Learn not to panic or quit if you run out of fabric for a particular plan. Look at it as an opportunity to be creative in quiltmaking and problem solving.

2. Relax about having "just the right amount." With so many variables, expecting to come out even is not realistic.

Fabric Preparation

To Prewash or Not to Prewash?

In a Nutshell

It's so easy to say prewash all your fabrics and just be done with it, but I don't do it or say it. In a nutshell, I pretest all fabrics as I select them for a particular project.

There are many reasons why I don't automatically wash all fabrics. The colors and the finish are more appealing to me before they are washed. I like the feel of the fabric better before it's washed. The crispness of unwashed fabric makes it easier to work with when using the machine techniques promoted in this book. To the contrary, people who only hand quilt have told me they think prewashed fabric needles more easily.

One of the interesting things to me is that as an antique quilt collector, I have observed that there are two things people find especially charming about antique quilts. One is the quilt or top that "has never been washed." The other is the quilt that has almost a puckered look because it shrank evenly and considerably when washed. Prewashing fabrics was not an historic thing to do. I pick my traditions carefully and if "they" didn't prewash fabrics, I don't need to either.

How to Test
I make 2-inch by 12-inch strips of each fabric I intend to use. I hold them under very hot water in the lavatory. If the color is going to run, you see it right there. Most bleeding is excess dye - that is, the dye is "spent" and will not permanently color another fabric, only the water - but you still need to deal with the fabric. Washing to get out the excess dye is the safest. Then test again.

When no color runs, I squeeze out the excess water and iron the strips dry. It is heat on the wet fiber that really causes the shrinkage. If any fabric shrinks beyond the 2 to 3% allowed by industry standards, I prewash that fabric or select another fabric. Two to 3% translates to $3/4$ inch to 1 inch in a yard or $1/4$ inch to $1/3$ inch in 12 inches. If one fabric shrinks considerably more than the others, it is a greater problem than if they all shrink the same little amount.

How to Prewash
Sort by similar colors and put fabrics in your washing machine. Use the dial to by-pass all steps except the last rinse and spin-dry cycles. Use cold water and no detergent; hot water is not necessary, and may promote color fading. (Although it is the heat on wet fibers that causes shrinkage, the dryer will be adequate for the job.) Detergent also facilitates color fading.

Then dry the fabrics in your dryer, but don't over dry. Press each piece with a steam iron. If any fabric is unusually limp, spray it with sizing (not starch) when you press.

Learning About Grainline

In a Nutshell

Crosswise grain, lengthwise grain and bias have three very different characteristics.

Lengthwise

The best way to study properties of woven fabric is by feel. With a piece of fabric about 18 inches square, preferably with one selvage intact, you can learn to identify grainline properties. Grasp the fabric with both hands on the selvage edge, positions A and B in **Diagram A**. Pull in opposite directions to make fabric taut. That's the lengthwise grain. The fabric has very little stretch in that direction, but it does have some stretch.

Crosswise

Now hold the fabric with one hand on the selvage and the other hand about 18 inches into the fabric, **Diagram A**, positions B and C. Pull again. Isn't that a surprise? That's the crosswise grain. With the same pressure, it will stretch two and one-half to three times farther than the lengthwise grain. Most commercial dress patterns suggest placement on lengthwise or crosswise grain. The inference is that they are the same. The fact is that they are not the same; the lengthwise grain is much firmer.

Bias

Bias isn't a four letter word. Well it is, but it's one you need in your sewing vocabulary, and you need to know how to use it! Go back to the 18-inch square of fabric and put your hands on opposite corners, **Diagram A**, positions A and C. Pull. Now that's stretch! Bias runs diagonally across the lengthwise and crosswise grains of the fabric, and is the most stretchy direction of a piece of fabric. There are times when that property will drive you crazy and times when it may save your project. The important thing is to understand it exists: it is a property of the fabric that does not change. Understand how to work with it.

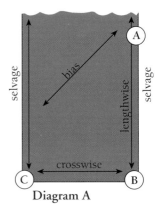
Diagram A

For starters, you need to know that you do not want bias on the longest dimension of a piece. You do not want it on the long outside edge of a block or a quilt where you will probably be adding borders or sashing next. But if you need flexibility and stretch, like on a narrow rolled binding along a scalloped edge, you'll bless bias.

Using Grainline Characteristics

In a Nutshell

Whenever possible put the longest outside dimension of a piece on the lengthwise grain. This includes strips! One of the things I am adamant about is the importance of cutting strips on the lengthwise grain. They are easier to work with, have smoother seams, press straighter, ravel less and printed patterns stay in line better. Please try it!

Strip Piecing and Grainline

When I started doing strip piecing, I cut across the fabric from selvage to selvage. It was the easy thing to do. Then I began to think about my training in garment construction and design. The lengthwise grain of the fabric was usually placed on the height of the body for good reason. Now, I stress using the lengthwise grain on the longest dimension of the cut piece whenever possible. Lengthwise grain on the long dimension of a border does much to add stability, especially if the item is intended as a wallhanging and has an obvious top. In patchwork being made into garments, whenever possible and when not contrary to the design statement, the lengthwise grain should run from head to toe.

In solid color fabrics, there is often a visible difference between pieces cut on the lengthwise grain and those cut on the crosswise grain. This is especially visible in larger pieces, such as plain squares that alternate with patchwork blocks.

Another important reason for cutting strips on the lengthwise grain revolves around the fabric problem called "bowing," **Diagram B**. That is the word used to describe the problem of threads being pulled out of position during the printing and finishing process. Crosswise threads, instead of being perfectly perpendicular to the selvage, are arched. If you then cut crosswise strips, you are cutting (breaking) every crosswise thread you hit. Everywhere threads are cut, they will ravel. (Theoretically, if you were

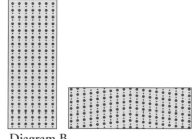

Diagram B

cutting crosswise strips, you would be cutting between two perfectly parallel crosswise threads and only cutting lengthwise threads.)

In addition, when fabric is bowed, any directional design in the fabric is pulled out of position, too. Cutting crosswise strips makes that distortion more obvious. Bowing barely effects lengthwise grain. Cutting strips on the lengthwise grain keeps printed patterns more accurate and greatly reduces raveling. Strips cut on the lengthwise grain will have smoother seams and be easier to keep straight while pressing.

So What's the Catch?

The catch is that if you are accustomed to buying only a quarter yard of fabric, the longest strip you can get is 9 inches. You can hardly call that a strip. That is why 27 inches (3/4 yard) has become my standard speculative purchase length. I have found that I much prefer the 27-inch strip to the 45-inch strip. (If by chance you have already calculated the number of 45-inch strips needed for certain quilt designs, just double the number for 27-inch strips. Yes, 27 doubled is 54, not 45, but sometimes the number of pieces you can cut from 27 inches is not as efficient as when cutting from 45 inches, so you may need the extra length.

This is not to cause you to become obsessed with the issue of lengthwise grain. Just try to think ahead. Before long, it becomes natural. There are times when the "trade-offs" required to cut strips on the lengthwise grain aren't worth it, such as:

1. Overriding design reasons. If the fabric has an obvious directional design that is an integral part of the design and contradicts the lengthwise grain choice—design is more important. **Example:** a printed stripe runs lengthwise. You want the stripe to go crosswise on the border for its dramatic effect. The longest dimension ends up cut on the crosswise grain - go for it!

2. Simple economics. You aren't willing to buy 3 to 3 1/2 yards of fabric 45 inches wide to cut four 3-inch wide borders on lengthwise grain. That's legitimate.

3. It's already sewn when you remember. You are the only one who can decide how big a problem something has to be before you rip.

Space and Tools

What About Your Work Space or Studio?

I highly recommend that you make quilts in the studio. You may physically be working on a folding table in the kitchen, but if you are mentally in "the studio" your results are definitely better.

A Design Wall

A design wall is a wonderful tool that can easily be set up in part of your studio. It can be as elaborate or as simple as your space and budget allow. The ultimate would be an entire wall of your studio covered with felt or bulletin board material, so you can position fabrics and stand back to study the effect. The simplest is a piece of batting temporarily taped to a wall or wrapped around a large bulletin board or piece of foamcore from the art supply store.

When selecting fabrics for the projects in this book, study the illustrations to determine the number of fabrics needed. Then experiment with your own fabric and color combinations. To help you decide on fabrics and positions, make a few samples and place them on your design wall. Stand back and look. Viewing the fabrics from a distance can make a tremendous difference in your selections.

The Sewing Machine

In a Nutshell

You really do need a sewing machine to take full advantage of the techniques offered in this series. Don't panic, you don't need a fancy machine. It must stitch forward. The tension must be properly adjusted.

If you haven't used your machine in a while, dust it off, clean out the lint, oil it, put in a new needle (size 14/90) and adjust the tension. If the tension is too tight, you can get seams that are puckered; if the tension is too loose, fabrics may actually pull apart so that stitches show through on the right side of the seam. Read your owner's manual for help.

Threads

Use good quality 100% cotton or cotton-wrapped polyester thread for the machine piecing. Don't be tempted by cheap thread. You will use lots of thread, but cheap thread is false economy. In most cases matching colors is not important, so you can sometimes find large spools of natural that will save money without compromising quality.

When it comes to machine quilting, I often use a very fine nylon transparent thread on the top of my machine with regular sewing machine thread in the bobbin.

In previous years, the name "quilting thread" was reserved for a heavier, usually waxed thread that came in limited colors and was designed for hand quilting. That kind of thread should be reserved for hand quilting and not used in a sewing machine. Now, however, there are some brands of thread called "quilting thread" that are unwaxed, and come in a multitude of colors. They are designed for both hand and machine quilting.

What Else?

Some Terms to Know as You Read This Book

Patchwork is easier when you are acquainted with these quilting terms.

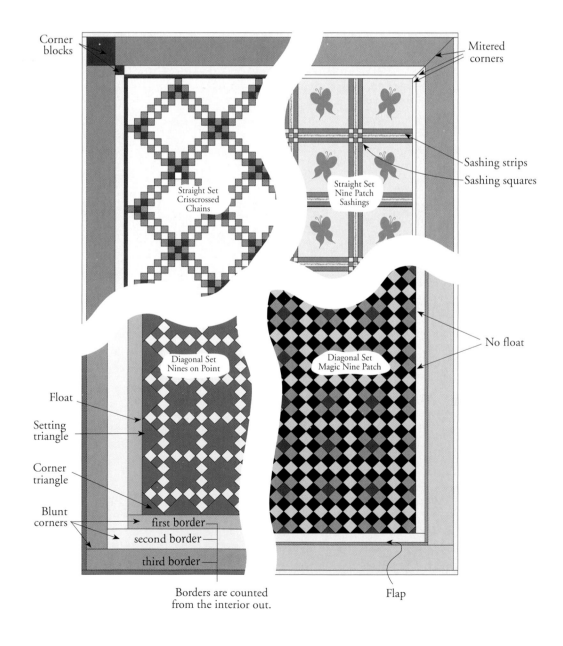

Corner blocks

Mitered corners

Straight Set Crisscrossed Chains

Straight Set Nine Patch Sashings

Sashing strips
Sashing squares

Diagonal Set Nines on Point

Diagonal Set Magic Nine Patch

No float

Float

Setting triangle

Corner triangle

Blunt corners

first border
second border
third border

Borders are counted from the interior out.

Flap

101 Quilts

Nine Patch Quilts - Straight Set

The Nine Patch quilts will be presented in three groups. The first group of Nine Patch quilts include those that are assembled in a straight set layout. Before you can make Nine Patch quilts, however, you must make Nine Patch blocks. Just in case you are new to quiltmaking, and strip techniques in particular, let's discuss making Nine Patch blocks using strip techniques. You may want to review the General Directions, pages 7 to 20 for information on cutting, pressing, the "second cut", and other general information on strip techniques.

Making the Nine Patch Unit

The most typical Nine Patch is a checkerboard with five squares of one color and four of a second contrasting color, **Diagram A**. This is sometimes referred to as the 5/4 plan. It is the style that will be used for these basic instructions. In most cases, strip sets for 5/4 Nine Patch units will not be included in the quilt diagrams that follow. However, when the Nine Patch block layout is unusual, either in size or color arrangement, you can expect to find strip sets diagrams on the specific quilt page.

Diagram A

Simply put, to make the Nine Patch, make a set of strips for each row, **Diagram B**. Frequently, Rows 1 and 3 are identical and one strip set can be used for both. If they are not identical, a strip set must be made for each row. If you are using directional fabrics, it is also a good idea to make three com-

plete strip sets. There is a more complete discussion of directional fabrics and Nine Patch blocks in Fenced-In Chickens, page 52.

Before cutting any fabric, think ahead and place the light and dark fabrics right sides together before cutting the lengthwise strips. You will have eliminated a step, and as a bonus, the strips will be more accurately positioned for sewing the seam.

1. Using **Diagram B** as a guide, sew the strips together into strip sets. Plan your pressing to create automatic pinning as discussed in Directional Pressing, page 11, either all in one direction or toward the darker fabric.

2. Place the strip sets for Rows 1 and 2 right sides together. Using the cut width of the individual strips as the increment length for the segments, make the second cut across the strip sets, **Diagram C**. Do not separate the pairs of segments after cutting: the

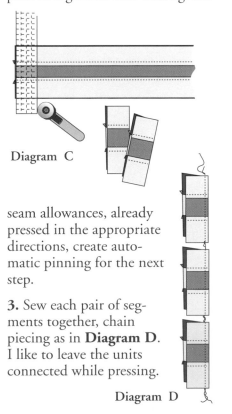

Diagram C

seam allowances, already pressed in the appropriate directions, create automatic pinning for the next step.

3. Sew each pair of segments together, chain piecing as in **Diagram D**. I like to leave the units connected while pressing.

Diagram D

Press either way, toward Row 1 or toward the center row, but generally you will want to be consistent.

4. Cut the last strip set into the same length segments for Row 3. Check and double-check that you are actually sewing Row 3 to Row 2! Then complete the Nine Patch unit by chain piecing the third row to the pairs, **Diagram E**. Remember, check and check again, it is really maddening to sew Row 3 to Row 1, **Diagram F.**

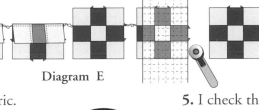

Diagram E

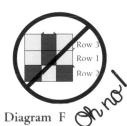

Diagram F Oh no!

5. I check the units individually by aligning perpendicular marks on an acrylic ruler with the seam lines, so that the edge of the ruler should match the edge of the unit. I check each unit against the MCM, and trim edges and threads and make minor cutting adjustments if needed.

When you start making Nine Patch blocks this quick and accurate way, you will love finding quilt designs that take advantage of your skills.

Combining the Nine Patch with Other Blocks

Many of the quilts in this book combine Nine Patch units with other blocks. For example, you will frequently see plain squares, the size of the finished Nine Patch, alternating with the Nine Patch units. Don't cut everything at once. When using strip techniques, the finished size of one sub-unit often determines the size to cut the next component. If the seam

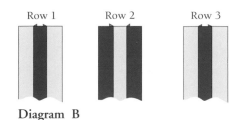

| Row 1 | Row 2 | Row 3 |

Diagram B

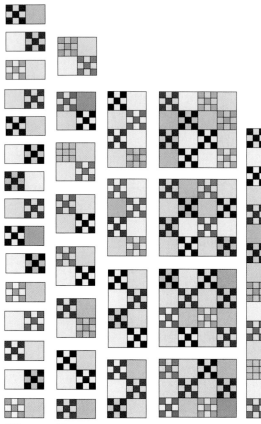

Diagram G

allowance you are using is slightly larger or smaller than 1/4 inch, the finished size of your sub-unit will be slightly smaller or larger than the mathematically correct measurement (MCM) for that sub-unit. You will learn that in most cases, your one and only (O&O) personal measurement replaces the MCM in subsequent steps. See page 10 for a discussion of MCM and O&O.

Assembling the Quilt Interior Using the Pairs Method

When assembling a quilt interior, there is a tendency to think that you will sew all the blocks in the first row together, then in the second row, etc., and finish by sewing the long rows together. However, it is easier to match seams when sewing pairs of blocks together, then pairs of pairs, then two pairs of pairs, etc., **Diagram G**. The reasoning behind this is that if all the blocks in each row were sewn together, then all the seam inter-sections have to match when sewing

the rows together. If a seam allowance is off anywhere, you will have to adjust continually along the seam. When sewing by the pairs method, many seams will only have one seam intersection to match, so that any discrepancies can fall into the seam allowances.

Arranging the Blocks

Do this step on the floor or a large design wall so the entire quilt interior can be seen simultaneously. Following the full quilt layout, arrange the blocks. Study the block assembly, and rearrange if necessary.

Putting Pairs Together

1. Take each block in the second vertical row and turn it face down on its partner in the first row, as if they were already hinged together. This puts them in the proper position for sewing.

2. Starting at the top of the quilt, pick up the pairs, maintaining the correct position by stacking them so that Pair #1 is on top of Pair #2, which is on top of Pair #3, etc. It's smart to pin a paper with each row number on the top pair as a reference as you handle the blocks, especially if you won't complete this step in one session, **Diagram H**.

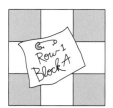

Diagram H

3. Hold the blocks in front of you, making sure you don't change hands or the position of the blocks! The "hinged" side must stay on the right, and Pair #1 on top! Go to the machine and start sewing the first pair.

As you finish the first pair, feed the second pair right under the presser foot, and then the third, etc. Do not

cut the pairs apart; the chain piecing will automatically keep them in the correct order.

4. When you have finished with vertical Rows 1 and 2, repeat with Rows 3 and 4, 5 and 6, etc.

Pairs of Pairs, Etc.

1. As you press the pieced pairs, you can create automatic pinning. On each pair, press the seam allowances so they alternate left and right down the row. You can feel the little ridge that develops as you press the seam allowance. Those ridges will act like little grippers as you put the pairs right sides together for the next seam. With a little practice, as you position the pairs, the ridges just meet, no space between, no overlapping, and no pinning necessary. The seam lines in the next seam will match perfectly.

2. Now sew the pairs of pairs. Four unit blocks are being sewn together, but there is still only one seam to match. Don't cut the thread keeping the vertical rows in line yet. It is more important to keep the positioning accurate than to take advantage of chain piecing, even though it means you need to handle each seam individually. If there is an odd number of rows in either direction, there will be one block left at the end.

3. Time to press again. Think ahead. If you press all of the seam allowances in Rows 1 and 2 up, 3 and 4 down, 5 and 6 up, etc., you will create automatic pinning for the vertical seams. All of this leads to a neat, flat quilt interior.

4. Now sew pairs of pairs of pairs together. There will be eight unit blocks and still only one seam intersection to match. Sew any extra pairs to the last group on each row.

5. Keep sewing larger units together until the interior is completely assembled. It may seem complicated now, but this planning becomes natural, and it is worth it in the orderliness that it develops and the problems that it prevents.

1 Nine Patch Sashings

Tip *For the Large Squares*

1. Use printed panels in every block.

2. Use Four or five panels balanced with a coordinating print.

3. Make appliqué blocks–four, five or nine, depending on when you tire of appliqué.

4. Photo transfer images provide lovely quilts to commemorate a special event.

5. T-shirts are wonderful for a memory quilt. Stabilize them with a very light fusible interfacing.

The finished size of this quilt is 49 1/2" (125.7 cm) square.
The finished size of the Nine Patch block is 3" (7.6 cm).

A successful adventure in Nine Patch quiltmaking can start with something as simple as four Nine Patch blocks accenting the triple sashing in a wall-hanging that features printed fabric panels.

The intricacy of one-inch squares in the Nine Patch blocks and matching one-inch strips for sashing creates the impression of thoughtful detail for what is a very simple quilt.

When planning your quilt, remember there should be good contrast between the background of the larger square and the sashing strips that surround it. So, if the background of the

square is light, the two outside strips of the sashing will be dark, and the center strip, light, as shown in the photo. It then follows that, as you keep alternating light and dark values, the Nine Patch will have five light squares and four dark.

Cut strips for the sashing, then sew the strips together to make a three-strip set. Press the seam allowances toward the darker strips. Cut the strip set into the lengths required to make the sashing units for your quilt. Cut four segments from these strip sets to set aside for Row 2 of the Nine Patches.

Make a short strip set for Rows 1 and 3. Cut eight and assemble the Nine Patch units.

Since the strip sets for the Nine Patch blocks are also pressed lighter seam allowances toward darker fabrics, the seams will match up automatically when the Nine Patch blocks meet the sashing units.

2 Nine-Sixteen

For more drama, surround nine or more blocks with Nine Patch sashing blocks and triple sashing. This is a lot more work: 16 Nine Patch units and 24 triple-sashing units, instead of four and 12. However, it is strong enough to balance a final border two to three times as wide as the one shown.

Tip *Changing the Proportions is Okay!*

The samples on this page show the block three to four times times larger than the triple sashing—the idea can be used with nearly any proportions. The key is to make the blocks dominant. They are the pictorial aspect of the quilt; the sashing is the frame. Cut some test strips before cutting everything else.

If this square is 1", the finished quilt size is 49½" square.
If this square is 2.5 cm, the finished size is 123.75 cm square.

3 Sixteen Nines

Reverse the values and add a third color to the Nine Patch to create another look.

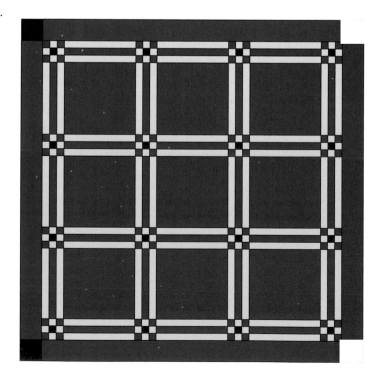

4 Spare the Nine Patch...

If this square is 1", the finished quilt size is 45" x 57".

If this square is 2.5 cm, the finished size is 112.5 cm x 142.5 cm.

5 ...Spoil the Child

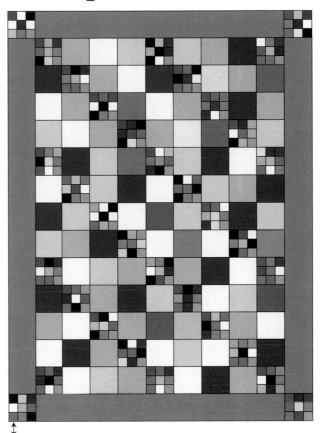

If this square is 1¹/2", the finished quilt size is 49¹/2" x 67¹/2".
If this square is 3.8 cm, the finished size is 123.8 cm x 168.8 cm.

Think Before You Start

Let's say you need a crib quilt in a hurry. You could make the quilt exactly as shown, above left. Drop 60 Nine Patch blocks (every little square finished to one inch) diagonally into a scrappy selection of 165 three-inch squares. The total number of pieces will be 705. All of a sudden you may think this is more work than you had in mind.

So instead, look at the quilt on the right. Select at least one print large enough to look great in finished 4¹/2-inch blocks. Cut the strips for the Nine Patch blocks 2 inches wide. Remember, each will finish 1¹/2 inches square, or 4¹/2 inches per Nine Patch. The quilt on the right will be slightly larger.

Did you count the units? This version requires only 34 Nine Patches and 87 squares, or a total of 393 pieces.

Go back to the drawing on the left. If the small square is 1¹/2 inches, the Nine Patch is 4¹/2 inches; if the quilt is 15 Nine Patches wide by 19 high, the quilt is 67¹/2 inches by 85¹/2 inches. Add an 8-inch border all around for a queen/double size quilt.

Tip *The Rule of Matching Corners*

Quilt 5 is the same as Quilt 4, with fewer blocks in each direction (and they are one and one-half times larger). I could have chosen other quilt sizes, but I wanted to include a Nine Patch in each corner–a quilt is usually more balanced when the corners match.

6 Nine Patch Trip Around the World

If this square is 1", the finished size is 87" square.
If this square is 2.5 cm, the finished size is 217.5 cm square.

Create a Nine Patch Trip Around the World by substituting Nine Patch blocks in some of the orderly rows of Trip Around the World.

Play the same "enlarge the Nine Patch" game you played on Quilt 4. To make Quilt 6, you need 156 Nine Patch blocks and 469 squares.

If every Nine Patch finishes at 3 inches, the quilt interior would be 75 inches square. Adding borders that are twice the width of a Nine Patch block brings the finished size to 87 inches square, which fits nicely below the pillows on several bed sizes. (See page 15 to review bed sizes.)

If a finished size of 80 inches would be fine, though, you could eliminate one row on each side and make 24 fewer Nine Patch blocks. This size would require 132 Nine Patch blocks and 397 squares.

Guess what—with Quilt 7, you can still make an 80-inch square quilt with even less work! If you increase the size of the smallest square by only one-quarter inch, the Nine Patch would then be 3³/4 inches square. Divide 80 inches by 3.75; the result is just over 21. You will need an odd number of rows in each direction for this design, so 21 is good. But because the border is the equivalent of two blocks wide, this slightly larger nine patch size requires an interior that is only 17 blocks square, which is outlined in white on Quilt 6. That is a total of 72 Nine Patch blocks and 217 squares.

You can easily manipulate many of the Nine Patch quilts in this book in the same way. We will not continue to remind you how easy it is to change sizes to suit your fabric choices, mood or time limitation on every quilt, but will do it occasionally.

7 Quick Trip Around the World

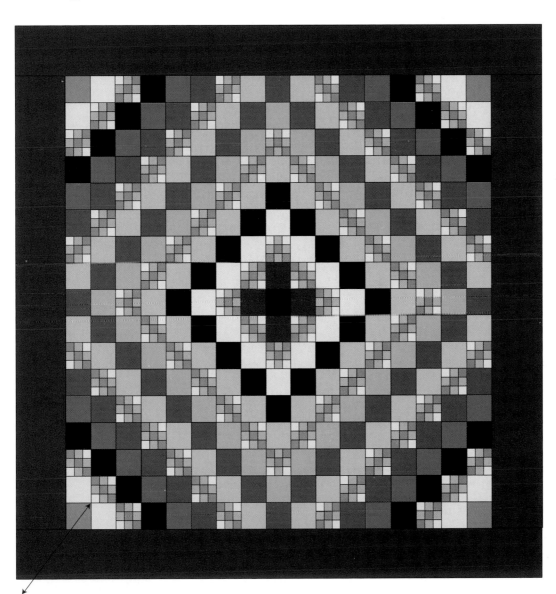

☐ If this square is 1¹/4", the finished size is 78³/4" square.
If this square is 3.1 cm, the finished size is 196.9 cm square.

8 Scrap O' Nine Tales

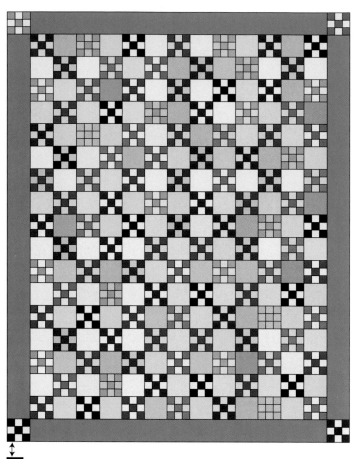

Nine Patch scrap quilts are a perennial favorite. The easiest version is the straight-set Nine Patch that alternates with plain squares. If dark fabrics are placed in the five position, use medium to light fabrics in the alternate squares. Likewise, if light fabrics had been placed in the five position, the typical arrangement would have dark fabrics in the alternate squares.

■ If this square is 1", the finished quilt size is 45" x 57".
If this square is 2.5 cm, the finished quilt size is
112.5 cm x 142.5 cm.

9 & 10 Not Scrap O' Nine Tales

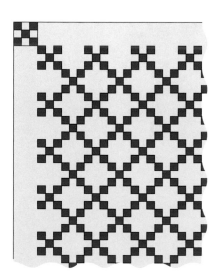

The same arrangement made with only two colors or even restricted to two fabrics, such as navy and off-white, will create an embedded look. This quilt is sometimes called a Single Irish Chain, but that name was reserved for Quilt 17 in this book.

Isn't it amazing how different these two look? Which do you like better?

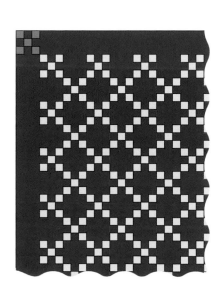

11 Scrappy Nines

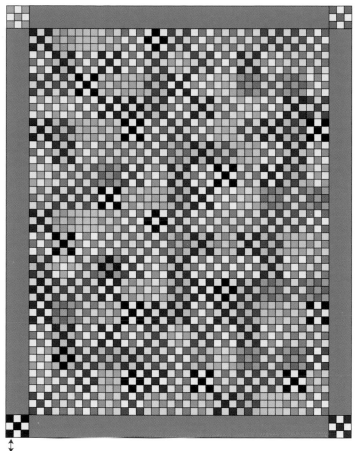

If this square is 1", the finished size is 45" x 51".
If this square is 2.5 cm, the finished size is 112.5 cm x 127.5 cm.

Another popular version is the side-by-side set, in which the Nine Patch blocks touch each other all over the surface of the quilt. To make this pattern work, you must make half the Nine Patch blocks with dark fabric in the five position and half with dark fabric in the four position.

Isn't it interesting how much smaller the Nine Patch pieces look in this version than in Quilt 8?

Since you press the seam allowances toward the dark fabrics when making the Nine Patch units, all seam allowances continue to alternate as the Nine Patches are assembled.

In the examples below, pressing all the seam allowances toward the darker fabric would create extra bulk where the seams intersect. The easiest way to solve the problem is to press all the seam allowances in the same direction, regardless of the fabric color. Rotate the strips as you sew the blocks together, so that the seam allowances on Rows 1 and 3 oppose Row 2. It may be necessary to rotate blocks as you sew them into rows, too.

12 Linked Scrappy

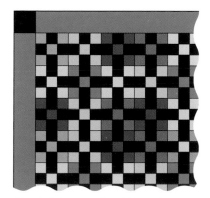

Dark fabric in the 4 position.

Another design option is to make all the Nine Patches with dark fabric in the same position. Dark fabrics in the four position create a strong appealing grid.

13 Blocked Scrappy Nines

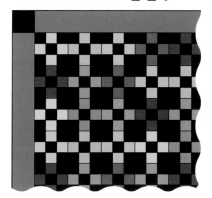

Dark fabric in the 5 position.

Yet when all the darks match in this arrangement, the result is blocky, not as desirable.

14 Changed My Mind Nine Patch

We pointed out in Quilts 4 and 5 that if you make the Nine Patch blocks larger, you won't have to make as many to get the same size quilt. This quilt is the answer when you decide that you're never going to make enough little 3-inch Nine Patch blocks for your quilt! Just change your mind and make the rest of the blocks 4½ inches square.

Instead of alternate squares to set these Nine Patch sub-units together, you will need alternate rectangles. The strips will be as wide as the small Nine Patch and as long as the large Nine Patch. If those rectangles match the color in the 4 position, the Nine Patch blocks will look embedded.

If this square is 1", the finished quilt size is 40½" x 51".
If this square is 2.5 cm, the finished size is 101.3 cm x 127.5 cm.

15 Changed My Mind Again

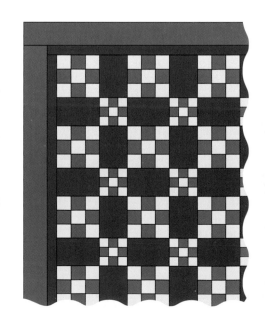

Take the same arrangement and add a third color for an entirely different look. This could also be very effective with scrap Nine Patches and consistent fabric in the rectangles or sashing strips.

16 Nine Patch Windows

If this square is 1", the finished quilt size is 41" x 50".
If this square is 2.5 cm, the finished quilt size is 102.5 cm x 125 cm.

Nine Patch Blocks

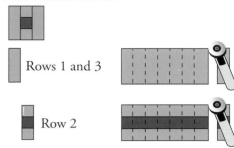

Rows 1 and 3

Row 2

Piece the strip set for Row 2 first and then cut Rows 1 and 3 the width of the Row 2 strip set. To cut Rows 1 and 3, cut across that strip in the same increment as the strips for Row 2.

These two-color Nine Patch Windows blocks could be made using nine squares of fabric. However, since all but the center square are cut from the same fabric, it is faster to construct the blocks using rectangles for the first and third rows and squares for the second row.

Make 154 two-color Nine Patch Windows blocks. Make all the centers scrappy like our example, or select one color to use consistently in all the centers. Set the blocks side by side, alternating the direction of the seams from block to block for flatter seam allowances. The inner border is

the width of one square. The outer border is the width of the Nine Patch Windows block.

17 Single Irish Chain

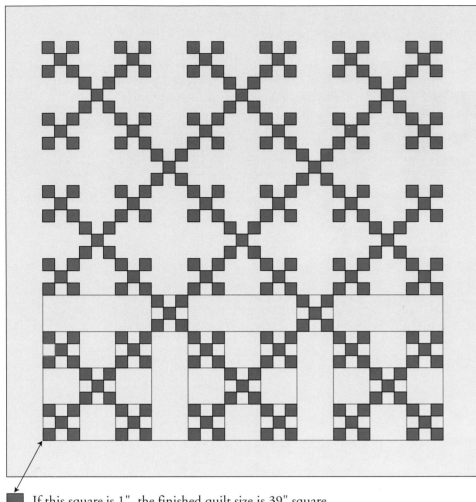

If this square is 1", the finished quilt size is 39" square.
If this square is 2.5 cm, the finished size is 97.5 cm square.

To make a Double Nine Patch block:

1. Make five 5/4-Plan Nine Patch blocks. Put dark fabric in the five-squares position.

2. From the light fabric, cut four squares equal in size to the Nine Patches made in Step 1.

3. Make a new larger Nine Patch with the five Nine Patch blocks and four plain squares.

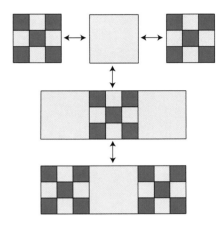

The light and dark positions can be reversed; it is important that the four squares in each Nine Patch, large and small, match. However, the five small squares in the small Nine Patch blocks can be scraps.

The quilt is called Irish Chain, or Single Irish Chain, when the Double Nine Patch blocks are set together with sashing the width of the small Nine Patch block, and small Nine Patch blocks are used as sashing blocks. It is a classic design.

Make a larger quilt by making the units slightly larger, and/or by adding more blocks, sashing and sashing blocks.

Light gray lines in the lower rows of blocks define the seam lines. Those lines barely show in a real quilt; they would distort the design if used throughout the diagram.

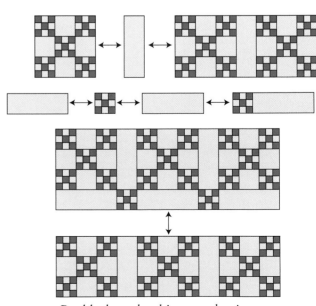

Put blocks and sashing together in rows.

18 Mismatched Double Nine Patch

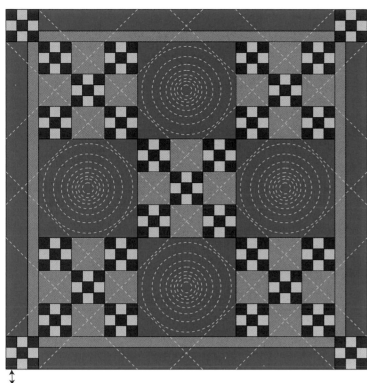

These double Nine Patch units do not have matching backgrounds like the classic arrangement described in Quilt 17, but they are still fun. This would be a good layout for framing printed panels or appliqué blocks, as shown in Quilt 1.

If this square is 1", the finished size is 33" square.
If this square is 2.5 cm, the finished size is 82.5 cm square.

19 Double Hopscotch

Substitute patchwork squares for the four large empty squares shown in Quilt 18, and add a few more Nine Patch blocks in the borders to create this fun Double Hopscotch.

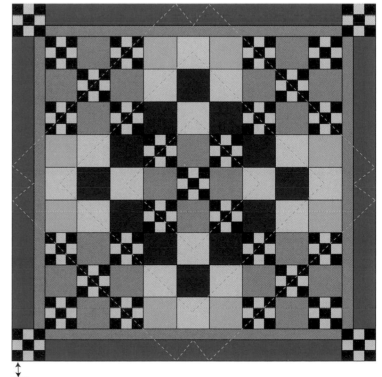

If this square is 1", the finished size is 33" square.
If this square is 2.5 cm, the finished size is 82.5 cm square.

Your Own Design(s)

A favorite design technique is the "what if?" game. What if I used red instead of green? What if I added an extra narrow border? Et cetera.

It would be terrific if this book had a centerfold so that you could look at the quilts on the next three pages at one time. You simply won't believe they are from the very simple grid below, in which Nine Patch blocks alternate with empty squares of the same size. You've already seen the result with scraps and two colors in Quilts 8, 9 and 10. Now for more variety in our orderliness!

You will want to make lots of copies of this page and play with colored pencils to create your own arrangement. You will be surprised how nice it is not to have a graph paper grid running through the unpieced square!

20 Argyle

Nine Patch Blocks

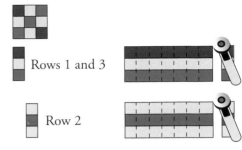

Rows 1 and 3

Row 2

Alternate Squares

Cut to match your O&O Nine Patch block size.

Double Nine Patch Blocks

Make 17

Note that Rows 1 and 3 are the same in all the Nine Patch sub-units, unless one of the fabrics is directional.

Make 18

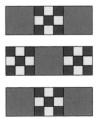
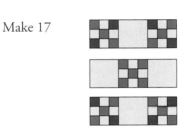

If this square is 1", the finished size is 51" x 69".
If this square is 2.5 cm, the finished size is 127.5 cm x 172.5 cm.

If this square is $1^1/2$", the finished size is $76^1/2$" x $103^1/2$".
If this square is 3.8 cm, the finished size is 191.3 cm x 258.8 cm.

Do you agree that this is a "guy" quilt? If you never knitted argyle socks for your honey, think how much more fun it will be to cuddle under an argyle quilt! See the sizes above. The $1^1/2$-inch or 4 cm strips will make a nice queen/double quilt. You may want to adjust the borders.

21 Spring Shadows

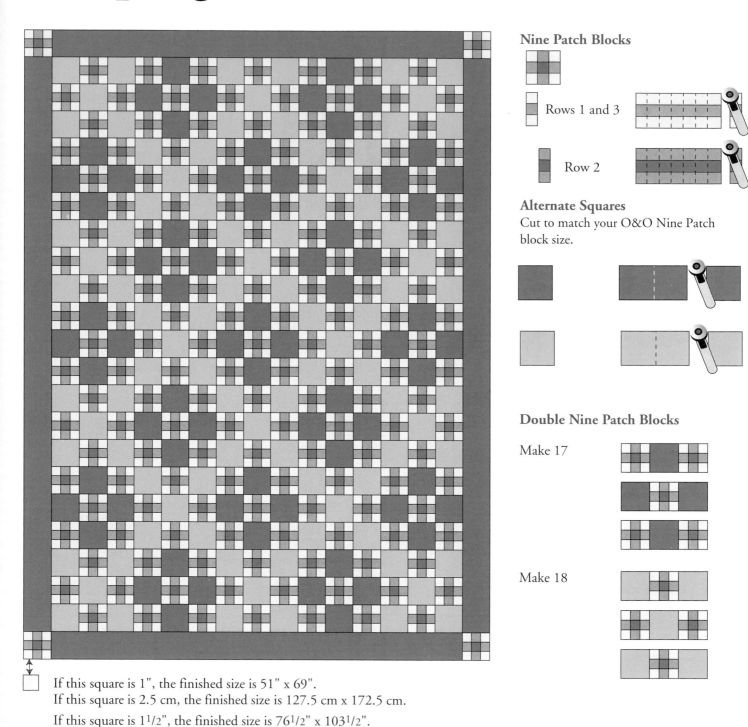

Nine Patch Blocks

Rows 1 and 3

Row 2

Alternate Squares

Cut to match your O&O Nine Patch
block size.

Double Nine Patch Blocks

Make 17

Make 18

If this square is 1", the finished size is 51" x 69".
If this square is 2.5 cm, the finished size is 127.5 cm x 172.5 cm.

If this square is 1^1/$_2$", the finished size is 76^1/$_2$" x 103^1/$_2$".
If this square is 4 cm, the finished size is 191.3 cm x 258.8 cm.

Out in the garden, all the Nine Patch
blocks are identical. They are set in
contrasting double Nine Patch layouts
that alternate across the body of the
quilt to make a terrific pattern.

22 Glendale

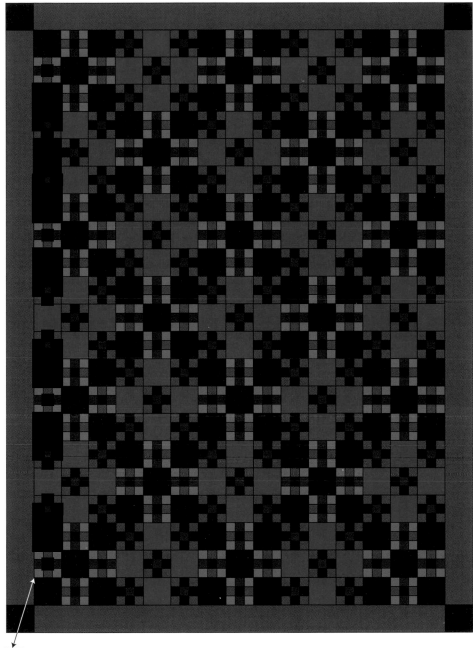

If this square is 1", the finished size is 51" x 69".
If this square is 2.5 cm, the finished size is 127.5 cm x 172.5 cm.

If this square is 1¹/2", the finished size is 76¹/2" x 103¹/2".
If this square is 4 cm, the finished size is 191.3 cm x 258.8 cm.

The consistent colors in the two small Nine Patch sub-units weave together this tartan of highly contrasting Double Nine Patch blocks. Be bold if you want this to work in your quilt.

Nine Patch Blocks

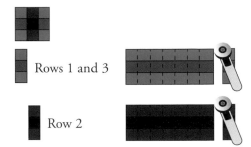

Rows 1 and 3

Row 2

Alternate Squares

Cut to match your O&O Nine Patch block size.

Make 18

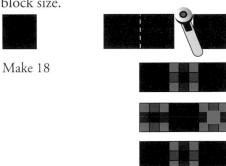

Nine Patch Blocks

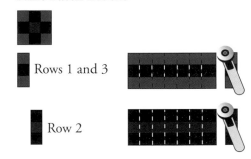

Rows 1 and 3

Row 2

Alternate Squares

Cut to match your O&O Nine Patch block size.

Make 17

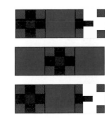

Crossword Puzzles

23 Sunday

If this square is 1", the finished quilt size is 69" x 80".
If this square is 2.5 cm, the finished quilt size is 172.5 cm x 200 cm.

In this design, we introduce a sub-unit that is even easier to make than the Nine Patch. Two strips are sewn together; one is the same width as the Nine Patch strips and one is twice as wide. Then the strip is cut into squares. This would be best described as a Modified Fence Rail block.

Cut this strip the same width as the strips for the Nine Patch blocks.

Cut this strip two times the **finished** Nine Patch strip width plus 1/2 inch.

In addition, there is considerable variation in the Nine Patch units. Instead of the typical 5/4 arrangement, the blocks for Sunday through Thursday emphasize a diagonal placement of matching squares with a secondary elbow arrangement.

Nine Patch Units for Sunday through Thursday

Make a separate strip set for each row, then cut the rows from the strip sets. Make this cut the same width as the strips were cut. The colors used in this illustration represent Sunday's Nine Patch.

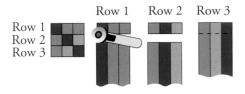

Nine Patch Units for Friday and Saturday

A different arrangement is needed for Friday and Saturday. You could say the Nine Patch units for Friday and Saturday are arranged in five diagonal rows, but still sewn in horizontal rows.

Friday's and Saturday's strip sets are:

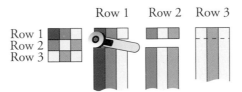

Selecting Fabrics

It is easy to see the endless possibilities once you identify the key sub-units, Nine Patch, Modified Fence Rail, center unit, sashing and sashing block, and you begin playing with the arrangement of values.

We've arranged just light, medium and dark values in very different ways. We stopped with only a week's worth of Crossword Puzzles, but I think we could have made a different one for each day of the year!

Spend some time looking at these illustrations; I think it will help you make fabric decisions. Monday, Tuesday and Thursday have very strong all-over diagonal patterns because the sashing blocks, center squares and diagonal in the Nine Patch all match.

The diagonal line of identical value is not broken.

However, look at Friday and Saturday. Rotate the Nine Patch ninety degrees, and the diagonal in the Nine Patch begins to echo the framed center square, almost making concentric circles contained in the sashing. Accent the "circle" by recoloring the Nine Patch as shown. The sashing blocks in both Friday and Saturday Crossword Puzzles are much more dominant than Puzzles from earlier in the week. The visual result is softer; the strong diagonal look is muted.

Other Sizes

Just another friendly reminder to think about changing the size of the strips to change the quilt size. If the strips for the Nine Patch are cut 1 3/4 inches wide rather than 1 1/2 inches, the quilt will be 86 1/4 inches by 100 inches.

24 Monday

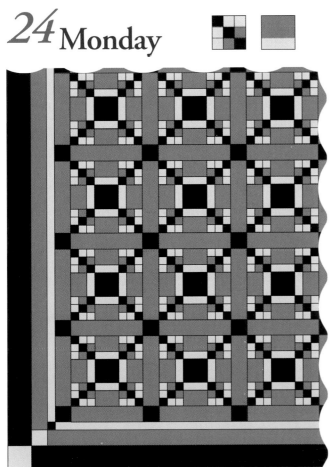

25 Tuesday

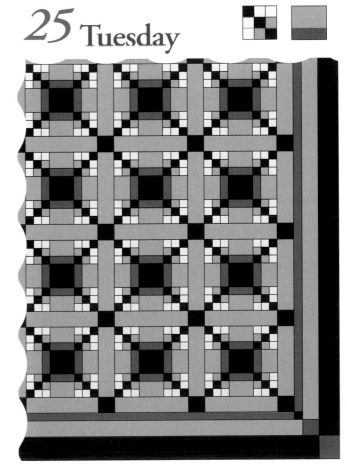

26 Wednesday

27 Thursday

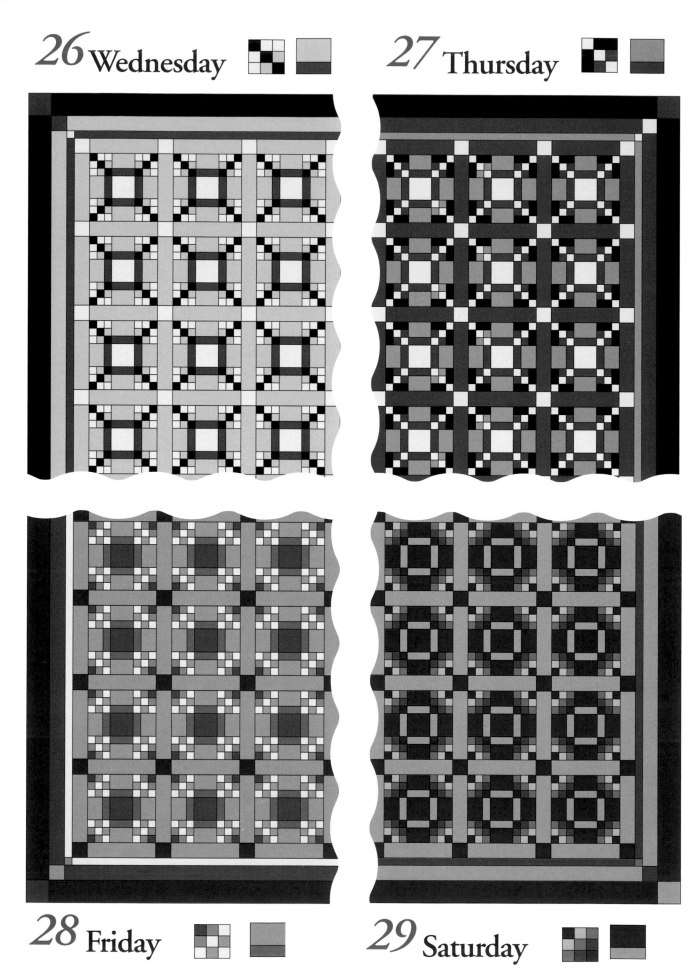

28 Friday

29 Saturday

Your Own Design(s)

The Crossword Puzzles designs are based on the grid shown below, as are the designs in the City Blocks series on the following pages. Use this grid to play the "what if" game and come up with your own design.

To color a new version for this series, photocopy the diagram and draw the appropriate lines in the sashing units.

We designed eleven quilts using this grid! How many designs can you come up with?

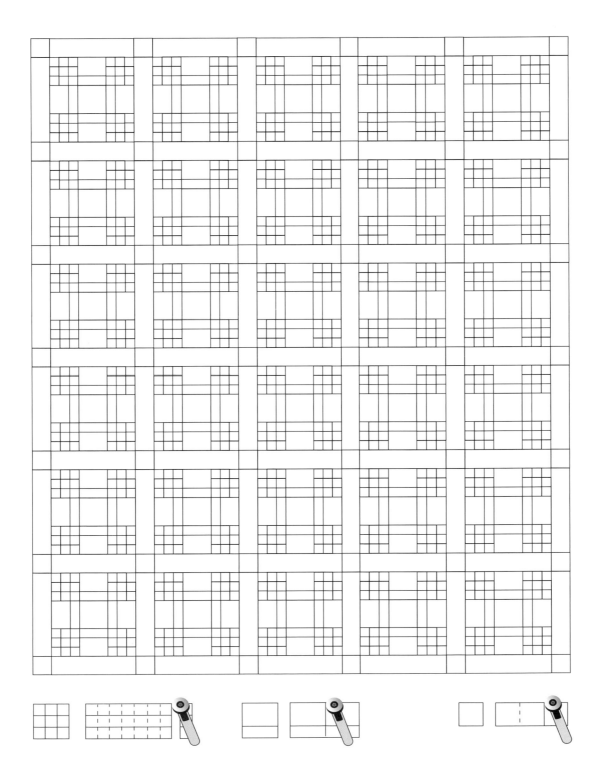

City Blocks Quilts

30 City Blocks

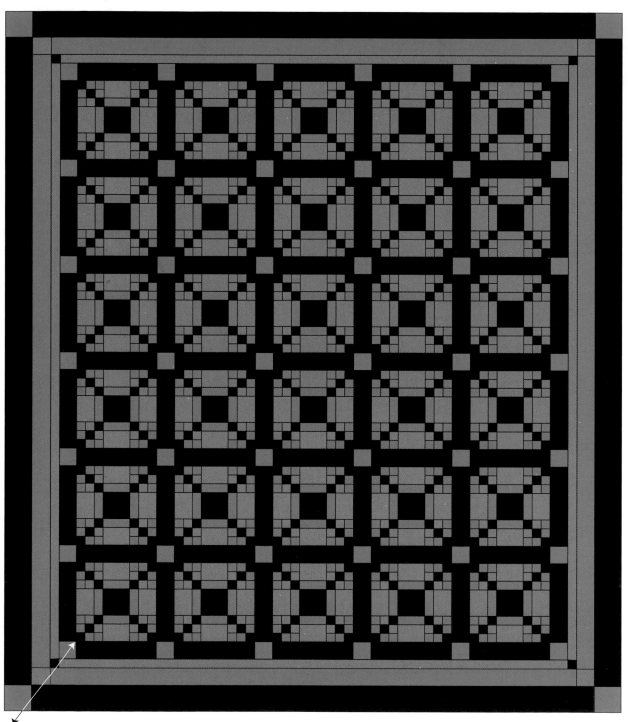

If this square is 1", the finished quilt size is 69" x 80".
If this square is 2.5 cm, the finished quilt size is 172.5 cm x 200 cm.

31 Uptown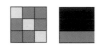

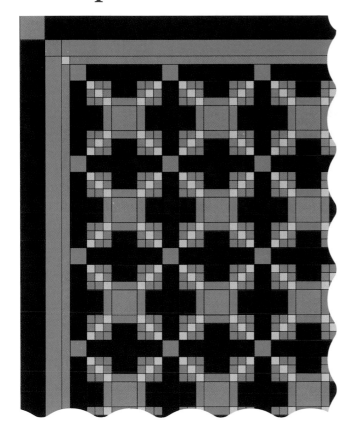

32 Midtown

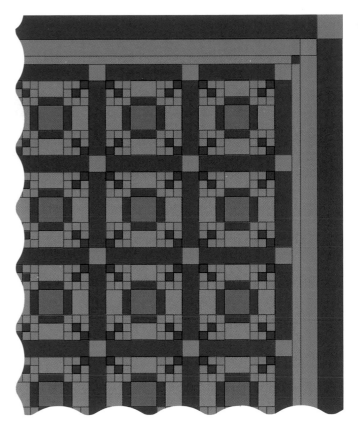

33 All Around Town

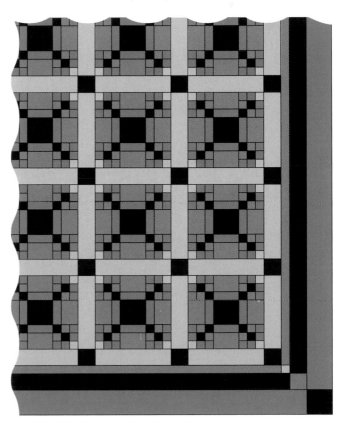

With an emphasis on sashing, Crossword Puzzles from the previous pages become City Blocks, and a new series of designs comes into being.

In addition to the dark sashing strips on Downtown, the high contrast between the sashing blocks and the sashing strips brings a focus to that intersection and the diagonal design remains secondary.

In Uptown, the sashing strips match the larger strip in the Modified Fence Rail sub-unit and create an entirely new shape, almost a basketweave look. Midtown and All Around Town have their own unique characteristics, as you should expect.

Isn't it fascinating that all of Crossword Puzzles and City Blocks are based on the same underlying grid?

34 Nine Patch Tiles

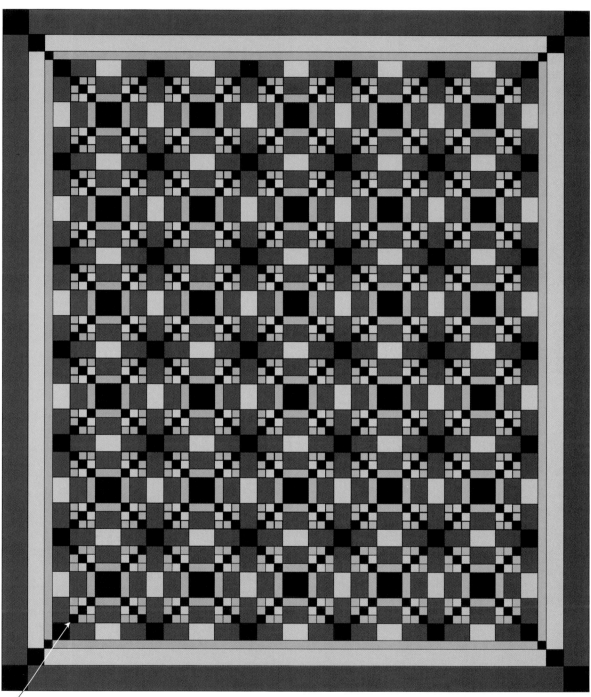

If this square is 1", the finished quilt size is 69" x 80". If this square is 2.5 cm, the finished quilt size is 172.5 cm x 200 cm.

If this square is 1$\frac{1}{2}$", the finished quilt size is 103$\frac{1}{2}$" x 120". If this square is 3.8 cm, the finished quilt size is 258.8 cm x 300 cm. For a size variation, see Nine Patch Tiles, Too, page 49.

35 Tiled Gridlock

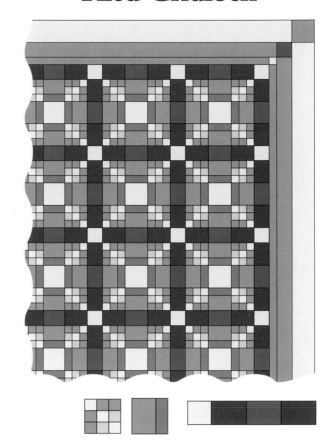

With a simple change in the sashing, Crossword Puzzles receives a new name, Nine Patch Tiles. The sashing, which had been the full length of the double Nine Patch section, is now divided into three equal-length pieces, each the length of a single Nine Patch sub-unit. This creates a new opportunity for strip techniques in your quiltmaking.

With a simple change in the placement of color values, you can achieve dramatic changes in the look of the finished quilt. No matter which quilt you are drawn to most, try to identify the parts of the design: sashing, sashing blocks, center block, frame around center, et cetera.

In this quilt I can easily identify eight different components. Think of the fabric choices as values from light to dark, not colors. Identify the proper value for each component in the quilt you like. No matter what color combination you want to use, do the same thing: Pick fabrics to match the values in relationship to each other.

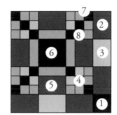

36 Parquet Tiles

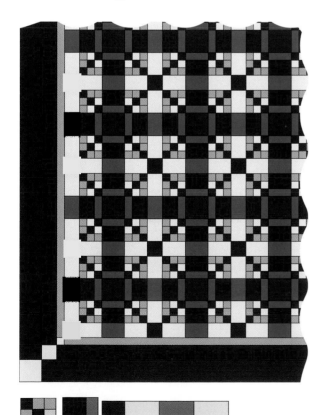

37 Sparkling Tiles

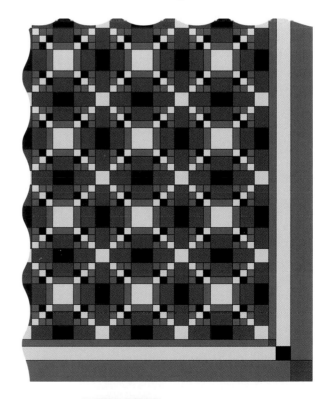

Strip Techniques for Sashing

Some people might cut three small rectangles for every sashing section and sew them together individually, but not us!

Make First Sashing Strip Set

Cut crosswise strips as wide as the Nine Patch is square. Yes, I said "crosswise," because when the sashing is finished, the longest dimension of each piece will be on the lengthwise grain. Cut one strip for each section of sashing. In all of our examples, that will be two of one color and one of the contrasting color. Sew them together as shown. Press the seam allowances away from the center of the strip set.

Add First Sashing to Block

Cut one sashing strip for every block, in your desired width. In the examples shown, the cut width of the sashing strips is equal to two of the smallest squares in the Nine Patch sub-units, plus seam allowances. Sew a strip in place along each block's lower side.

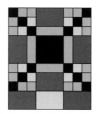

Make Second Sashing Set

Sashing squares separate the pieced sashing strips where the corners of four blocks meet. Instead of cutting individual sashing squares, your next trick is to include a strip for the sashing square with the strip sets you make for vertical sashing strips.

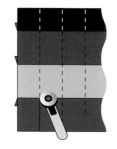

From the sashing square fabric, cut a strip the same width as the sashing strips were cut. Make strip sets as shown.

Add Second Sashing to Block

Cut one sashing-and-square strip for every block and sew to each block's right side. Also cut one sashing-and-square strip for each horizontal row, one for each vertical row, and a single sashing square. For Quilt 34, that means 11 extra sashing strips. These 11 sashing strips and one sashing block will complete the left side and top edge of the quilt. Add additional borders to complete the quilt.

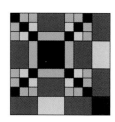

What a Difference 1/4-inch Makes!

Crossword Puzzles, City Blocks, Nine Patch Tiles and all of their variations were diagrammed on the same basic grid. If the smallest square in the Nine Patch blocks equals one inch, the finished quilt would be 69" x 80".

Remember, we are not recommending a one-inch grid for every quilt, just giving you a basic size. If you make 1 1/4-inch finished squares for the Nine Patch in any of these quilts, and make the sashing and borders proportionate, the quilts would be 86 1/4 inches by 100 inches, a great queen/double size.

Before you start cutting, think about 1 1/2-inch finished squares for the Nine Patch. A 1-inch square is great for a wallhanging, but 1 1/2-inch squares are probably as small as you want for a bed quilt. Make any of those quilts with 1 1/2-inch finished (2 inch cut) strips and the quilt would be 103 1/2 inches by 120 inches–suitable for a king size quilt, way too big for a queen/double.

Cutting bigger pieces usually can reduce the number of pieces which should mean you can finish sooner. This quilt is no exception. You can eliminate a row of blocks in both directions and the last row of sashing; that saves 538 pieces. If you make the square 1 1/2 inches and the borders proportionate, the new quilt, Nine Patch Tiles, Too, will be approximately 81 inches by 99 inches.

38 Nine Patch Tiles, Too

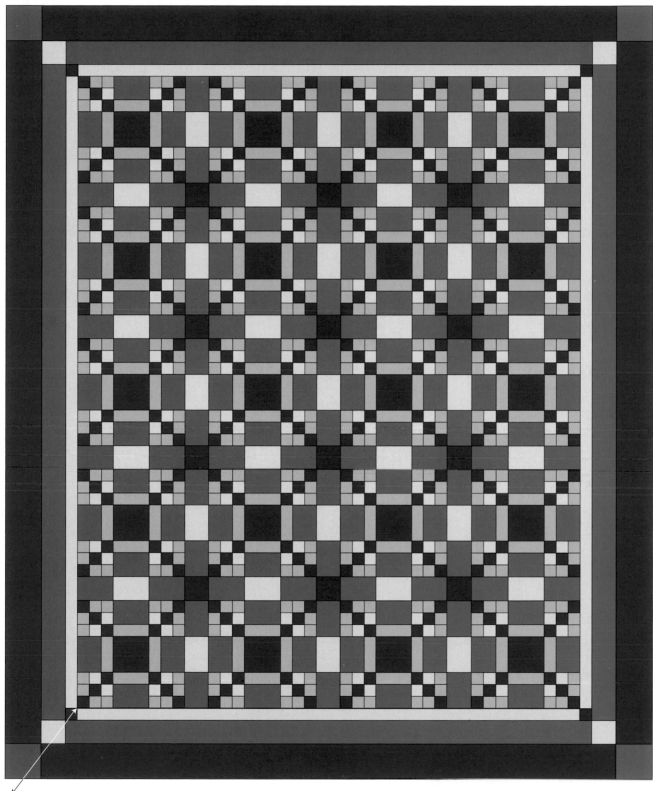

If this square is 1", the finished quilt size is 54" x 66".
If this square is 2.5 cm, the finished quilt size is 135 cm x 165 cm.

If this square is 1¹/2", the finished quilt size is 81" x 99".
If this square is 3.8 cm, the finished quilt size is 202.5 cm x 247.5 cm.

39 Twice as Much Fun

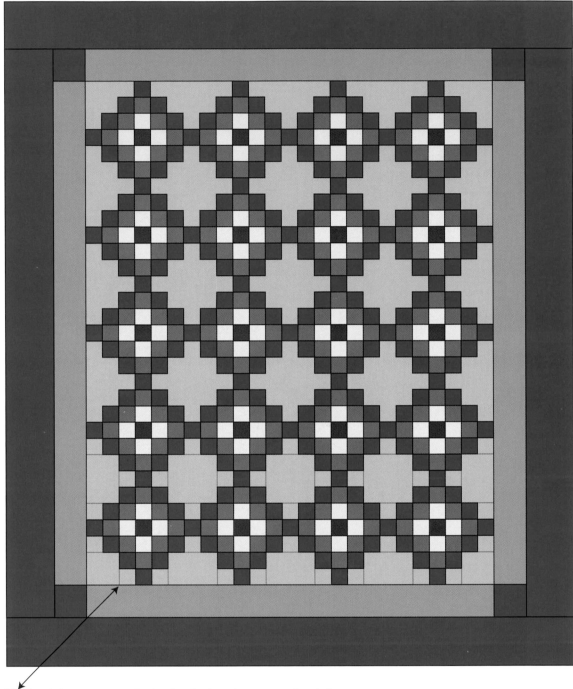

 If this square is 1", the finished quilt size is 35" x 41".
If this square is 2.5 cm, the finished size is 87.5 cm x 102.5 cm.

On page 23, we talked about the 5/4 checkerboard design. Both blocks shown below fit that description. When

I combine both styles of Nine Patch blocks, I call it Twice as Much Fun. In addition, there is nothing that requires Nine Patch blocks to be made with just two fabrics. You might say that increasing the number of fabrics is Twice as Much Fun, Doubled!

Just look at the examples on the next page. While playing around with the Nine Patch on graph paper, I started doodling with the pattern from page 34 that we sometimes call Single Irish Chain and ended up with a design reminiscent of an Album block.

Imagining the Quilt

I started doodling with the Single Irish Chain pattern:

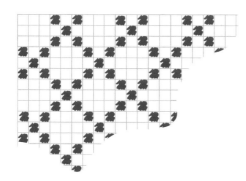

Adding the opposite Nine Patch (four dark/five light) inside every other big diamond looked nice:

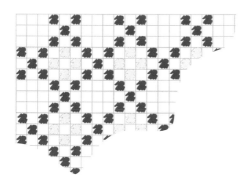

The obvious thing to do next was to make a concentric diamond in a third color and add a contrasting center:

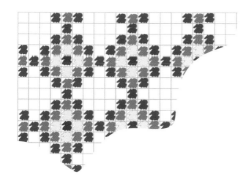

Finally, I eliminated one row of the outer Nine Patch units to make the overall pattern more pleasing.

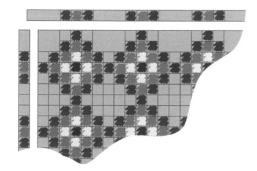

Now the design looks more pleasing. I also liked the fact that it looked complex, but the construction would be easy. Make partial Nine Patch blocks to complete each side.

Making the Quilt

Nine Patch Block 1 is a 4/4/1 arrangement.

Nine Patch Block 2 could be called a 5/2/2 arrangement, not previously used.

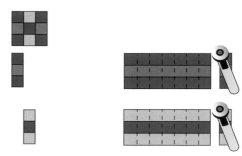

In addition, there are alternate unpieced units…

and partial blocks…

that make the surprisingly simple but attractive quilt.

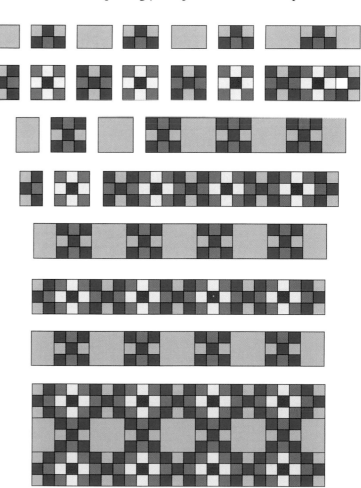

40 Fenced-In Chickens

The finished quilt size is 37¹/2" (93.8 cm) square.
The finished size of the Nine Patch block is 4¹/2" (11.4 cm).

This quilt made by Gudfinna Helgadóttir is a great lesson in how using directional fabrics can reduce the efficiency of strip techniques—and at the same time, a good example of why directional fabrics can be worth the effort.

In addition to choosing directional fabrics, which dramatically reduces efficiency, the nine 4/4/1 Nine Patch units are all different. The units for Row 2 must be cut individually so that all the center squares can be different. So, while the scrap Nine Patch units enhanced the charm of the quilt, they certainly reduced the use of streamlined techniques like chain piecing.

On the next page, you will find some discussion of directional versus non-directional fabrics and a chart that details the units required for using both types of fabric.

Refer to the chart on next page to position the Nine Patch blocks, partial blocks and unpieced units in their proper positions for stitching into rows.

Selecting Fabrics

Some of the most wonderful fabrics, like the chicken print in Gudfinna's quilt, are directional. Some fabrics have a very subtle directional overtone that you don't even notice until you spot one or two squares out of 50 that are "different!" Actually, the green print in this quilt is one of those. You probably can't tell it in the picture, and I won't dwell on it in this discussion, but this fabric has a subtle chicken wire look. Even though it is obvious that it would add to the confusion, the fabric was just too perfect for the quilt to substitute something else.

This discussion is not meant to say, "Don't use directional fabrics when using strip techniques." It is written with the goal of saying, "Know what you are doing when you choose directional fabrics." Clearly, the inference is, "When you need real speed and the benefit of strip techniques, don't select directional fabrics."

Efficiency Comparison

Non-Directional Fabric	Directional Fabric
Sub-unit A 9 scrap Nine Patch centers	Sub-unit A 9 scrap Nine Patch centers
Sub-unit B 12 connecting Nine Patches just alike	Sub-unit B 6 connecting Nine Patches just alike
	6 connecting Nine Patches
Sub-unit C 4 large unpieced squares	Sub-unit C 4 large unpieced squares
8 unpieced rectangles	4 unpieced rectangles
	4 unpieced rectangles
4 smaller corner squares	4 smaller corner squares
12 partial blocks (Rows 1 & 2 of connecting Nine Patches)	3 top units of connecting Nine Patches
	3 bottom units of connecting Nine Patches
	3 left units of connecting Nine Patches
	3 right units of connecting Nine Patches

41 Sticks 'n Stones

The finished quilt size is 82¹/4" x 100¹/4" (205.6 cm x 250.6 cm).
The finished size of the Nine Patch sub-unit is 4¹/2" (11.4 cm).

This design is similar to Twice as Much Fun. One horizontal row consists of Nine Patch and Fence Rail units; the other row is made of squares and Fence Rails.

To make a full-size quilt as shown, cut the Nine Patch and Fence Rail strips 2 inches wide. Cut the alternate blocks 5 inches wide. Assemble the sub-unit into rows to create illusions of circles.

Nine Patch Blocks

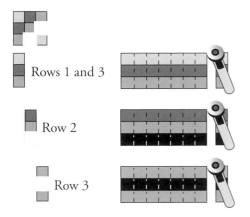

 Rows 1 and 3

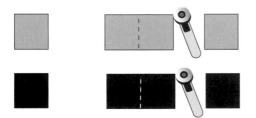 Row 2

Row 3

Fence Rail Blocks

Cut the strips the same width as the strips for the Nine Patch blocks.

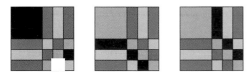

Alternate Blocks

Cut to match size of unfinished Nine Patch blocks.

Make these four unit blocks…

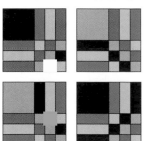

to make one master unit.

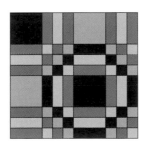

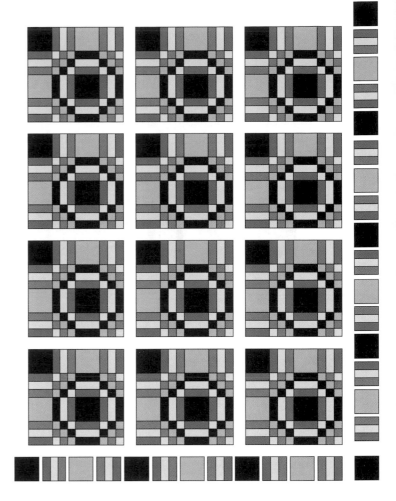

See how different the quilt looks when the arrangement is slightly changed and the circles are touching the sides of the quilt. One-inch cut strips made this a 20" (50 cm) square quilt.

42 Irish Sticks 'n Stones

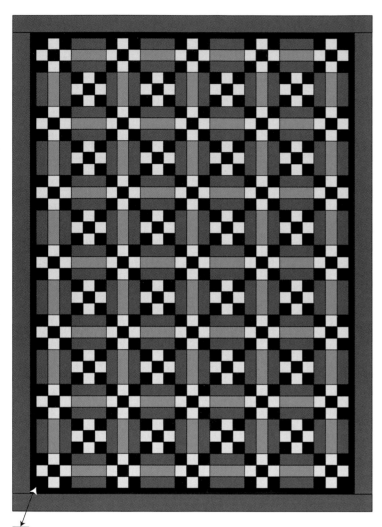

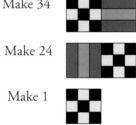

Nine Patch Blocks

Make 59

Rows 1 and 3

Row 2

Fence Rail Blocks

Make 58

Cut to match unfinished Nine Patch blocks.

Make 34

Make 24

Make 1

If this square is 1", the finished quilt size is 33" x 45".
If this square is 2.5 cm, the finished size is 82.5 cm x 112.5 cm.

Since Nine Patch and Fence Rail blocks have combined so well in several quilts, let's try another combination. It is really easy because all of the Nine Patch units match and the Fence Rails are the same fabrics. Just alternate them across the quilt. I think you will like this quilt best with Nine Patch units in every corner. On the first row, the Fence Rail units are horizontal, and on the second row, they are vertical. Alternate from row to row, but stop with a horizontal row for the best balance.

The recommended construction is not rows, but pairs, pairs of pairs, et cetera, as discussed on page 24.

If you like this quilt, you will probably like its diagonally set cousin, Main Streets, on page 109.

Tip *Think Ahead*

Practice on a couple of strip sets and make a decision about directional pressing. You may prefer pressing all seam allowances in the same direction rather than "toward the darker fabric."

43 Framed Nine Patch

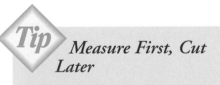
If this square is 1", the finished size is 29" x 39".
If this square is 2.5 cm, the finished size is 72.5 cm x 97.5 cm.

Nine Patch Blocks

Rows 1 and 3

Row 2

Frame
Cut strips the same width as the strips for the Nine Patch blocks.

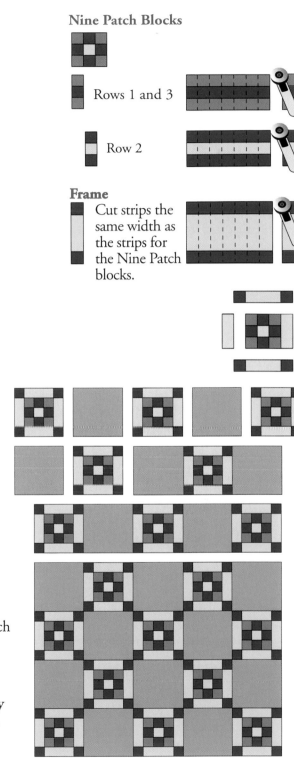

Eliminate a few strips on Irish Sticks 'n Stones and you will see the Framed Nine Patch.

Tip *Measure First, Cut Later*

Wait to cut the plain alternate blocks until you know whether to use the MCM or O&O size (page 10).

Don't cut all the center strips on the frame pieces until you have completed the Nine Patch units. Then cut the strips the width of the unfinished Nine Patch.

Use this block to accent lovely appliqué pieces (see page 58).

44 Framed Nine Patch with Alternate Appliqué Blocks

If this square is 1", the finished size is 33" x 43".
If this square is 2.5 cm, the finished size is 82.5 cm x 107.5 cm.

Check Out the Nine Patch Border!
To make the Nine Patch border, you can use completed Nine Patch units and piece them together, or just keep alternating Rows 1 and 2.

45 Fields 'n Fences

Tip *Create Sewing Simplicity with Disappearing Seams*

Sew a few seams in the fabric you choose for the ecru position to check for a disappearing seam quality. Make another choice if necessary.

If this square is 1", the finished quilt size is 35" x 47".
If this square is 2.5 cm, the finished size is 87.5 cm x 117.5 cm.

If you think this is a framed and sashed Nine Patch, wrong! The simplicity of the construction of this quilt will make you groan! Look at the top part of the diagram. Now, look at the gray seam lines we've added at the bottom.

Use a sufficiently busy print, and with almost the same layout as Sticks 'n Stones, you create a quilt that looks like a Framed Nine Patch set together with sashing and sashing blocks. Instead, you have the simple Fence Rail and Nine Patch again.

The only difference is that partial blocks are used to complete the illusion of frames and sashing pieces before the border is added.

46 Independence Square

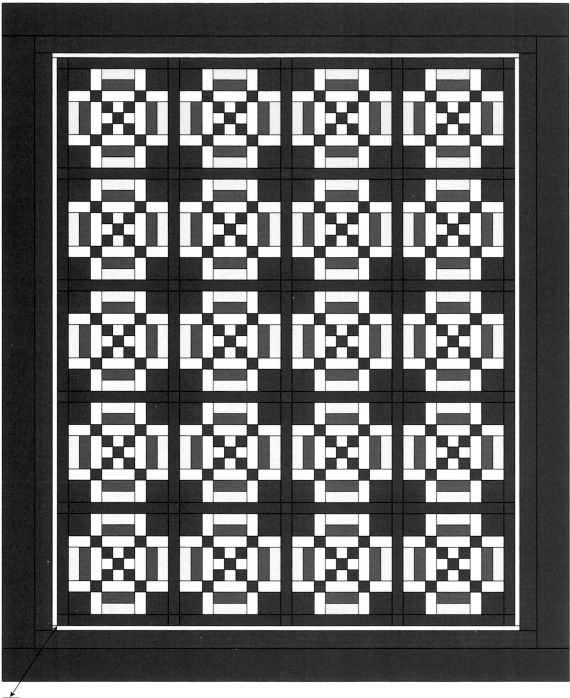

■ If this square is 1", the finished size is 51" x 61".
If this square is 2.5 cm, the finished size is 127.5 cm x 152.5 cm.

If you don't show your friends the breakdown for this quilt, they'll never guess how easy it is to make! The blocks, or master units, of this quilt are made with three very simple blocks, or sub-units.

When the blocks are set together with a narrow sashing, the result is one terrific quilt!

Sub-units

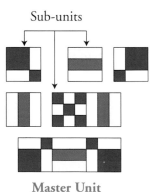

Master Unit

The first thing to do is decide on the size of the finished squares in the Nine Patch center block. Every other strip size is dependent on the Nine Patch strips.

 The Nine Patch sub-unit is the classic 5/4 arrangement.

 The Fence Rail blocks are three strips sewn together and cut into squares.

 The Modified Nine Patch could be defined as an Irregular Four Patch, but we're not going to do that because we are basing the size on the center Nine Patch.

The Modified Nine Patch could be made with nine small squares created with these three strip sets:

Rows 1 and 2 are alike.

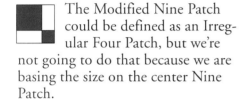

Do you think it makes sense to cut a strip for each row and sew them together when you could just cut a bigger piece? Of course not!

Double-check what size that bigger size is before you cut. If each finished row is supposed to be 1 inch, and you were cutting individual strips, each strip would be $1^1/2$ inches wide to include two $1/4$-inch seam allowances. To get the right size for the bigger strip, multiply the number of rows (2) by the finished size (1 inch) and then add the two $1/4$-inch seam allowances ($2^1/2$ inches).

A common mistake for beginning strip-technique quiltmakers is to double the cut strip width ($1^1/2$ inches doubled is 3 inches). Don't get trapped!

Use the same reasoning to figure out the cut size of the white strip in Row 3.

The narrow sashing and sashing block are also cut the same size as the strips in the Nine Patch.

Modified Nine Patch Blocks

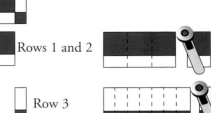

Rows 1 and 2

Row 3

Think Smaller

On several quilts, the idea of enlarging pieces has been developed. With this quilt, I encourage you to think of $3/4$-inch finished strips. The majority of the pieces are much larger, but the use of the small pieces in the center Nine Patch focal point of each bock will give the illusion that the whole quilt is equally as intricate!

Nine master units would make a great wallhanging about 30 inches square.

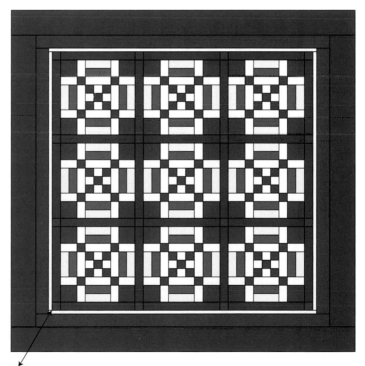

If this square is $3/4$", the finished size is approximately 32" square.
If this square is 1.9 cm, the finished size is approximately 80 cm square.

Your Grandmother's Irish Chain

The classic Double Irish Chain is made with two alternating unit blocks. You can see how they repeat at the bottom of the quilt diagram.

Each unit is five units wide by five high, or what I call the 25 Patch block. It is a wonderful design, popular and well-recognized.

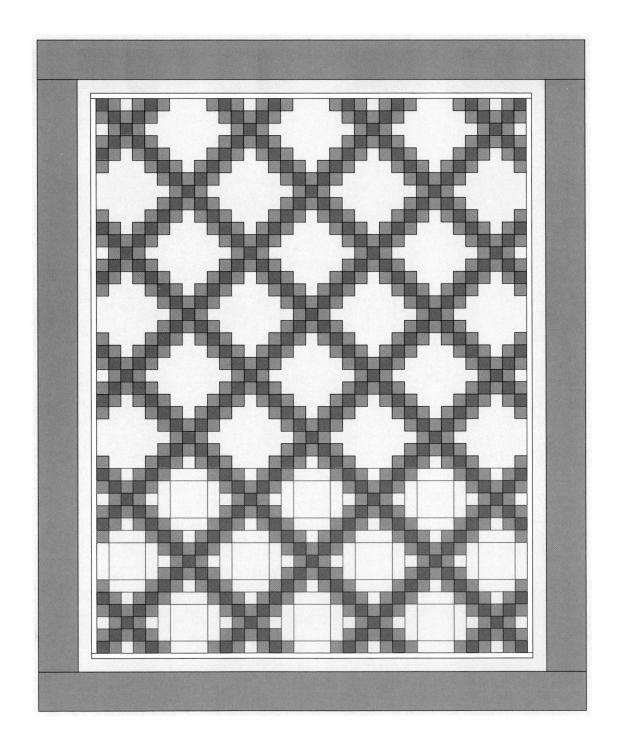

47 Not Your Grandmother's Irish Chain

Do you have a really good friend who drives you crazy because she's always correcting you about names of quilts? Well, flash this quilt at her! She'll swear it's a Double Irish Chain and you can drive her crazy for a change!

While not made using the classic Double Irish Chain technique, the next four quilts will make you think Double Irish Chain quicker than a leprechaun can disappear. So, come along, my lads and lassies, and see how Nine Patch blocks can help you

make these quilts in the twinklin' of an eye!

All the quilts share the same secret block. Turn the page to learn the secret.

If this square is 1", the finished size is 53" x 65".
If this square is 2.5 cm, the finished size is 132.5 cm x 162.5 cm.

First, the secret: The Nine Patch way to make an Irish Chain-style quilt.

The master unit is similar to a Double Nine Patch. The variation is that the four squares in the center of each side include one row of smaller squares. Those rows would all be made from the same strip set and, in this case, that strip set matches Row

2 of the Nine Patch blocks in the corners of the master unit.

But that's not all–the blocks are set together with sashing and sashing blocks that match the center.

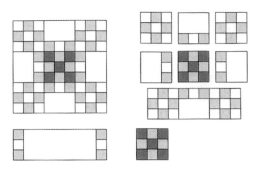

48 Crisscrossed Chains

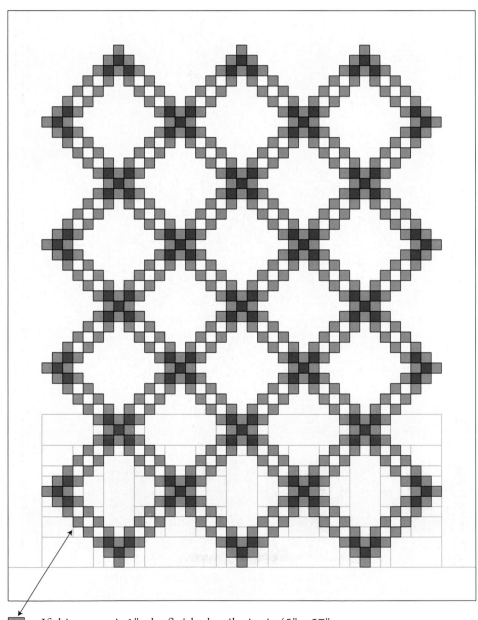

If this square is 1", the finished quilt size is 45" x 57".
If this square is 2.5 cm, the finished size is 112.5 cm x 142.5 cm.

Designing Crisscrossed Chains

This is a perfect example of the effectiveness of design by omission. By omitting some of the squares in the outer rows, the remaining squares frame themselves rather than push the edge. The look is quite different. The borders are the width of a Nine Patch unit. Make them twice as wide

and you create room for a beautiful quilted design in the border.

Making the Crisscrossed Chain
The key to taking advantage of the efficiency of strip techniques is to break the quilt down into repetitive units. Once you have determined what the sub-units are, you can count the number needed. Then make all of the same units at one time.

In addition to the eight large master units in this quilt, there are eight partial units that create the edge. The count is continued on the next page.

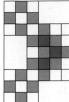

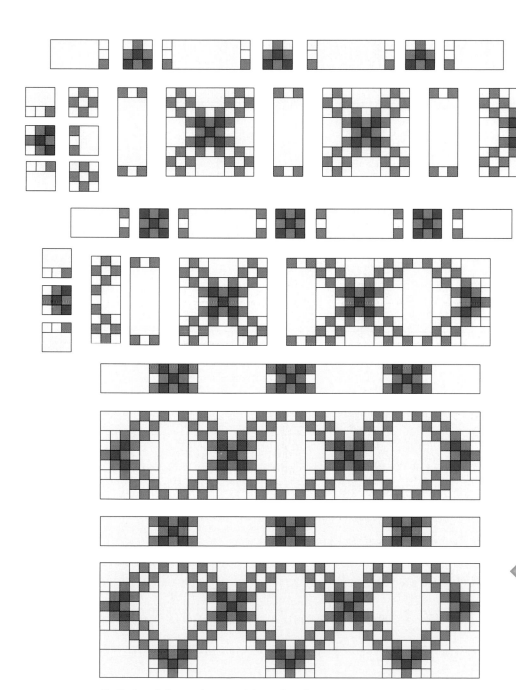

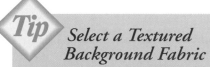

Quilt breakdown shown without borders.

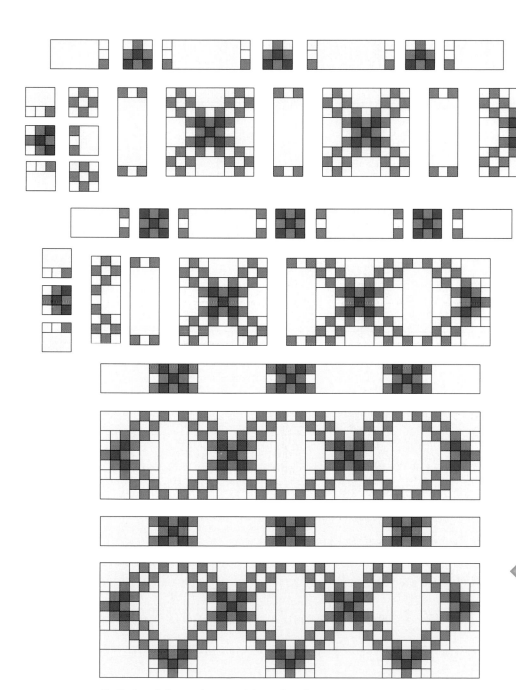

Tip *Select a Textured Background Fabric*

To create a continuous look across the background area despite the seams that occur, choose a small textured tone-on-tone print.

Crisscrossed Chains — Key to Sub-units

Sub-unit	No. to Make	Used In	Tips and Comments
A	17	Master unit and sashing blocks.	Standard 5/4 Nine Patch.
B	48	Corners of master unit and partial master units.	Standard 5/4 Nine Patch.
C	40	Center sides of master unit and partial master units.	Pieced strip set same as Row 2 of Nine Patch in B.
			You can now make 8 master units. You will have these sub-units remaining: 9 16 8
D	14	Partial master units, top and bottom rows of the quilt.	Rows 2 and 3 are the same as in the center Nine Patch. Row 1 matches Row 1 in the Corner Nine Patch. The strip sets can be cut and sewn at the same time.
E	16	Partial master units.	
			You can now make 8 partial master units. You will have 6 remaining D sub-units for the top and bottom rows of the quilt.
F	18 (6 horiz. 6 vertical)	Sashing in center section.	Center section is as wide as the O&O Nine Patch measurement and as long as 7 finished pieces of the master unit plus 1/2 inch for seam allowances.
G	4	Sashing in top and bottom rows.	End pieces match those in E.
H	6	End pieces on horizontal sashing rows.	End pieces match those in F.
I	2	Top and bottom rows.	End pieces match the pieced strip set in E.
J	2	Top and bottom rows.	End pieces match the pieced strip set in E.

49 A Hug and A Kiss

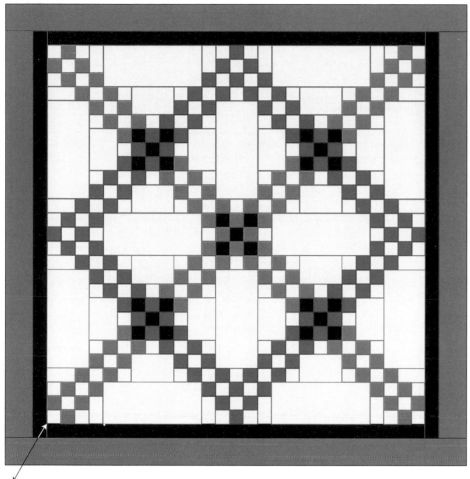

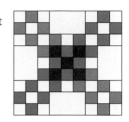

Master Unit
Make 4

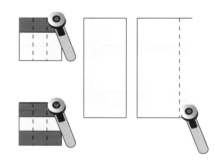

You can use the same strip set for sub-units B and D. Just reverse half of the strips when stitching.

The long sashing pieces are the length of seven finished small squares plus 1/2 inch for seam allowances.

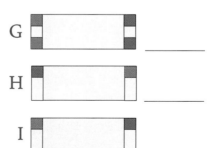

If this square is 1", the finished quilt size is 33" square.
If this square is 2.5 cm, the finished size is 82.5 cm square.

Now that you've looked at the breakdown of Crisscrossed Chains, why not practice the same process with this small wallhanging? We've added a second color in the chain. Here are the 9 sub-units.

How many of each do you need?

A  _____

B  _____

C  _____

D  _____

E  _____

F  _____

G _____

H _____

I _____

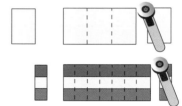

Answers: A: 12; B: 8; C: 12; D: 12; E: 4; F: 1; G: 4; H: 4; I: 4. Have fun!

50 Celtic Chain

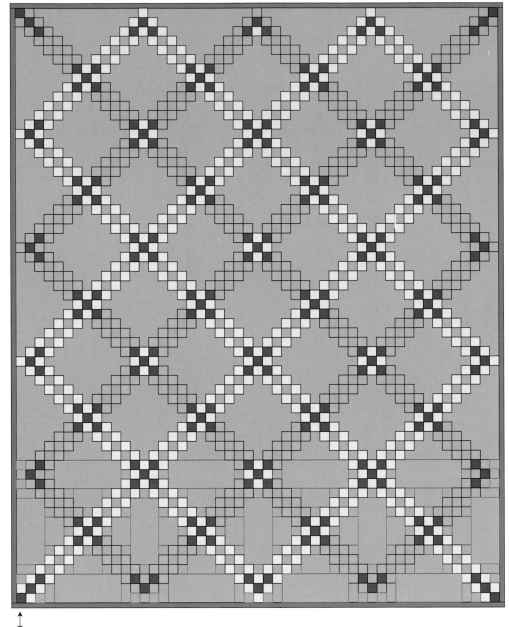

If this square is 1", the finished quilt size is 51" x 63".
If this square is 2.5 cm, the finished size is 127.5 cm x 157.5 cm.

Keep growing A Hug and A Kiss and you can create Celtic Chain. The master unit is the same. The more you look at this block, the more fun it is!

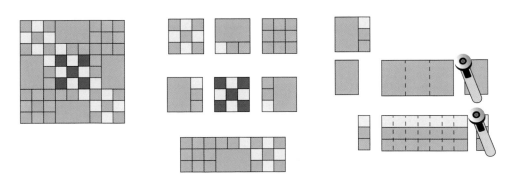

51 Celtic in the City

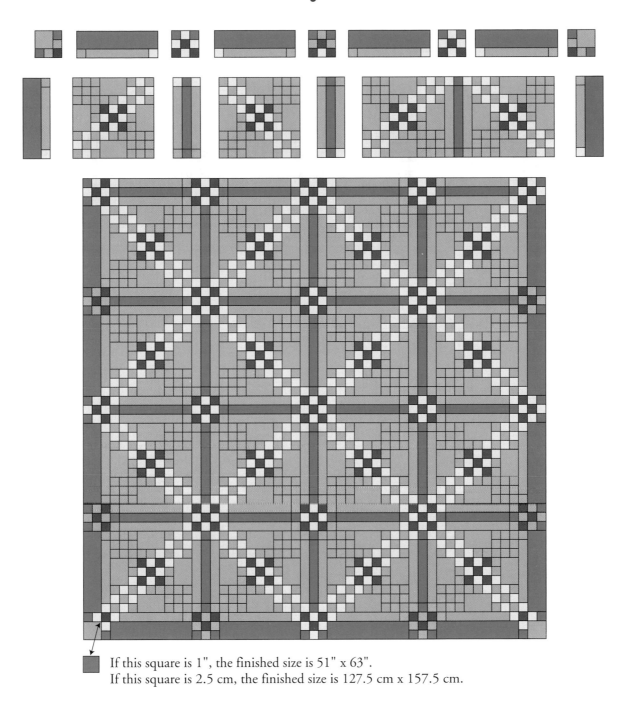

If this square is 1", the finished size is 51" x 63".
If this square is 2.5 cm, the finished size is 127.5 cm x 157.5 cm.

You say you want a little more activi-
ty? Use this sashing unit
in the interior of Celtic Chain,
and this unit
on the outer edge of the quilt. Complete the transformation with four
cute corner blocks. What an amazing
difference!

52 Confetti Chain

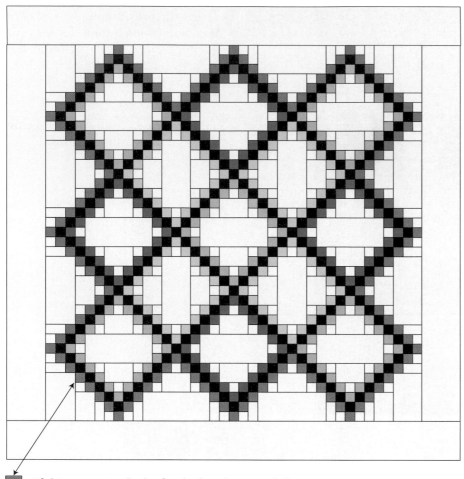

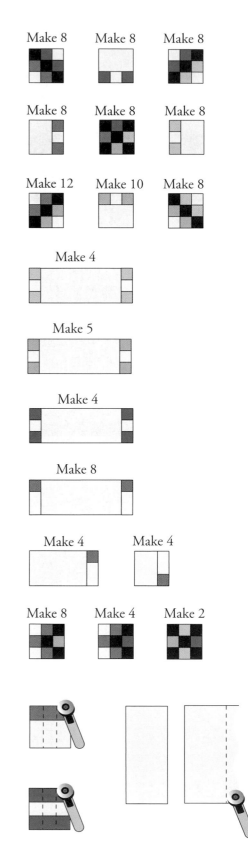

Make 8 Make 8 Make 8
Make 8 Make 8 Make 8
Make 12 Make 10 Make 8
Make 4
Make 5
Make 4
Make 8
Make 4 Make 4
Make 8 Make 4 Make 2

If this square is 1", the finished quilt size is 47" square.
If this square is 2.5 cm, the finished size is 117.5 cm.

Just like confetti, let's put some more colors into the mix. We've included the grid so you can easily see the sub-units. It looks so complex but, one little unit at a time, it's a snap.

Master Unit

There are six master units in the Confetti quilt shown above, so you might think you will just have to make six of everything – but wait! Many of the same sub-units are used in the remainder of the quilt. You can still take advantage of the efficiency of strip techniques on this simple but very complicated looking quilt.

The nine Nine Patch sub-units required to make the master units are shown at the top of the page. Six of each of those units are used to make the six master blocks; the remainders are used in the sashing strips and on the edges of the quilt interior.

53 Amish Confetti Chain

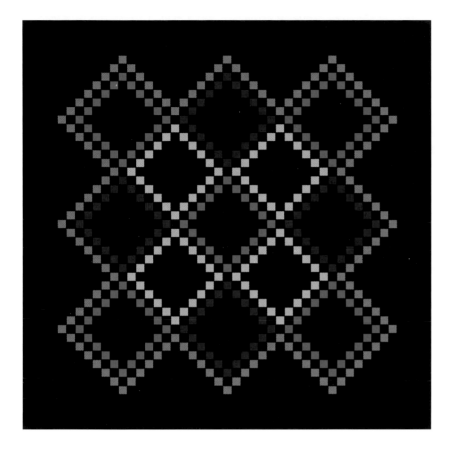

Change the background to black and the four colors to jewel tones for a dramatic difference. Since the background and the square in the center of the chain match, each square of color looks individually embedded in the block.

Substitute the sub-units shown below, or color your own using the grid.

Make 8   Make 8   Make 8

Make 8   Make 8   Make 8

Make 12   Make 10   Make 8

Make 4

Make 5

Make 4

Make 8

Make 4   Make 4

Make 8   Make 4   Make 2

Design Your Own

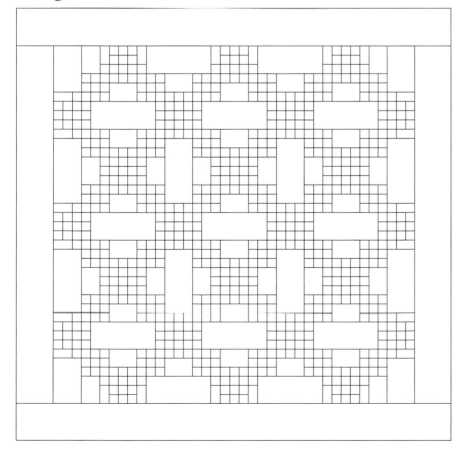

54 Nine Patch Propellers

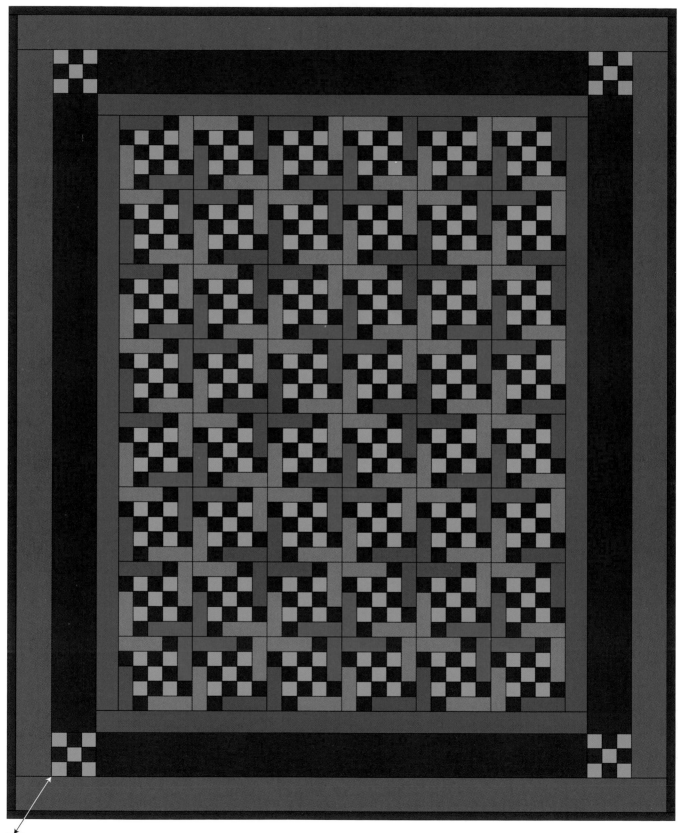

If this square is 1", the finished size is 45" x 55".
If this square is 2.5 cm, the finished size is 112.5 cm x 137.5 cm.

In addition to being very graphic, Nine Patch Propellers is a good introduction to blocks made with a partial seam.

Rotating one block is all that is required to create the alternating propeller colors. The block combines a basic Nine Patch with flying squares and strips (propellers) in three fabrics.

Partial Seam Technique
To avoid a set-in seam when adding the last strip-and-square, use a partial seam when adding the first strip-and-square.

1. Start with the Nine Patch and the strip-and-square that will be added to its right side.

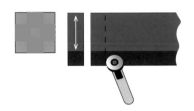

The square should align with the last row in the Nine Patch. With right sides together, begin sewing about halfway down the length of the Nine Patch, and sew to the end of the strip-and-square. Leave the upper end of the strip loose.

2. Working clockwise around the Nine Patch, sew the three remaining strip-and-square combinations in place, stitching the entire seam for each one. Match the square and Nine Patch seams carefully. Press seam allowances toward the Nine Patch.

3. After adding the final strip-and-square, go back to the first strip and complete the partial seam.

Make 48 blocks

Lay them out in 12 sets of four, rotating blocks 90 degrees counterclockwise, as shown.

Try other combinations of colors and layouts on the grid diagram below.

Tip *Grain Teaser*

The lengthwise grain of the propeller piece will run in the longest dimension of the piece if you make the first cut for these strips on the crosswise grain.

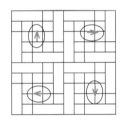 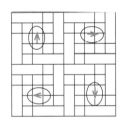

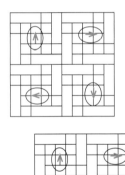

Design Your Own

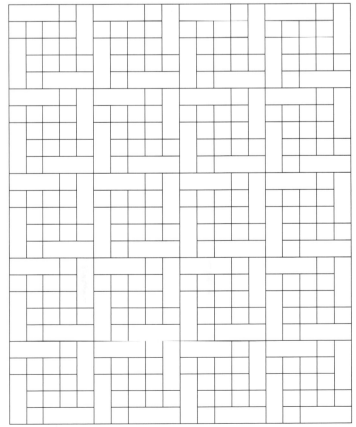

55 My Favorite Squadron

The finished size of this quilt is 39" (97.5 cm) square.
The finished size of the unit block is 7¹/₂" (18.8 cm).

This wallhanging was planned in colored pencil to use just one block like Nine Patch Propellers. In the small wallhanging size, I didn't like the center propeller colors at the edge of the quilt. Substituting a third fabric in the edge position meant I had to make four different sub-unit blocks, but it seemed justified.

Select two fabrics that contrast strongly with each other and with the Nine Patch fabrics for the alternating propellers. A subtle low-contrast fabric is nice for the propeller strips that create the border. Make the basic Nine Patch blocks.

Cut strips for the propellers and flying squares on the crosswise grain. Propeller strips are cut as wide as the finished Nine Patch, including seam allowances. Strips for the flying squares are cut the same width as the strips for the Nine Patches. Make strip sets from each combination of fabrics for the strips and squares. Cut across the strip sets in increments the same width as used when making the Nine Patches. Assemble four of each of the four blocks. Join the blocks into sets of four, stacking them as shown. Rotate each set of four blocks in the direction shown and join.

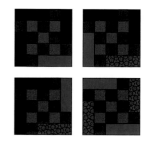

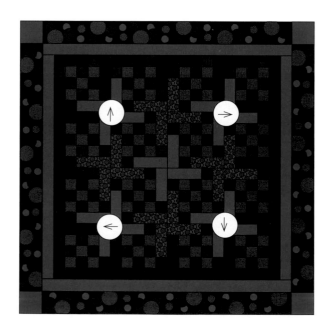

Nine Patch Quilts - Diagonal Set

Up to this page, all of the Nine Patch quilts shown have been straight set. That means the quilt block is resting flat on one side. When the blocks are tipped or set on point instead of resting flat, it is called a diagonal set.

It is said in design that there are only three basic shapes: the square, the circle and the triangle. Reduced to its simplest interpretation, squares are rigid, circles are restful, and triangles are dynamic. Diagonal lines equate with triangles; that is why they almost always result in a more interesting quilt.

When you are working with diagonal set quilts, you may have to tilt your head or turn the book or quilt so you can see the unit blocks in flat rows. When you set blocks on point, you will see that there are triangles at the end of each diagonal row. They are called Setting Triangles.

One of the easiest ways to maximize your results for the time spent is to work with designs that feature strong diagonal lines. Many of the previous quilts, even though straight set, feature a diagonal design line and have a dynamic look. See Crossword Puzzles (page 40), Crisscrossed Chains (page 64), Celtic in the City (page 69) and Not Your Grandmother's Irish Chain (page 63) as examples. Other times it is necessary to position the unit blocks on point to create a diagonal design line.

In this section, you will learn the Secrets of the Setting Triangles. Corner Triangles are also needed for diagonal set quilts. While the triangles look alike, they aren't. That is another secret.

Occasionally there will be a notation to compare a quilt in this section with one in the section on straight set quilts. It is always surprising how little resemblance there is between a straight set design and the same design set on point.

56 Nine Patch Chain

The finished size of this quilt is 18¹/₂" x 22¹/₂" (46.3 cm x 56.3 cm).
The finished size of the Nine Patch block is 3" (7.5 cm).

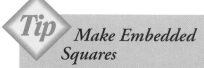 **Tip** *Make Embedded Squares*

The small white squares appear to be embedded in the blue background. That great effect is created by using the same fabric in the alternating square as in the four squares of the Nine Patch.

In its simplest form, the diagonal set Nine Patch makes a most appealing quilt. The light fabric in the five position of the 5/4-Plan Nine Patch in the photographed quilt appears embedded because the alternating squares are the same fabric. This also creates a secondary shape in the quilt.

Light fabric in the four position and and matching light alternate blocks makes Quilt 57 a reverse Nine Patch Chain.

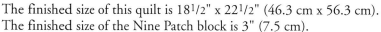

The two quilts on this page show only two fabrics plus borders, but read on—there is no reason, except personal preference, to limit yourself to just two fabrics.

57

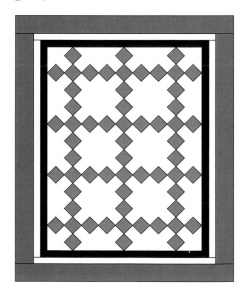

The Nine Patch Chain Gang

58a
58b
58c

In these three versions of Quilt 58, the contrasting color of the alternate non-pieced blocks creates a new pattern that highlights and defines the Nine Patch blocks. The interior alternate blocks could be the perfect spot for some fancy quilting, signatures, photo transfers, et cetera.

Smart Border
What a great border with the smaller

Nine Patch blocks on Quilts 59 and 60! Don't think of this as a separate border; it is just a continuation of the patchwork. Make the finished strips for those blocks one-half of the size of the strips for the larger Nine Patch. The new small block fits into larger pieced blocks and pieced setting triangles. And, again, what a difference there is between the two- and three-color versions.

Don't Forget Templates
If you are fortunate enough to own some of the From Marti Michell Perfect Patchwork Templates Sets, they include many of the triangles commonly needed. For example, for a 3-inch finished Nine Patch, Set A Triangle #2, cut with the hypotenuse on straight grain, is the perfect setting triangle size. Also see pages 78 and 79.

59

If this square is 1", the quilt is 50½" square.
If it is 2.5 cm, the quilt is 126.3 cm square.

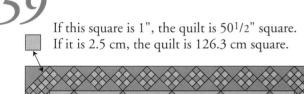

60

If this square is 1", the quilt is 25½" square.
If it is 2.5 cm, the quilt is 63.8 cm square.

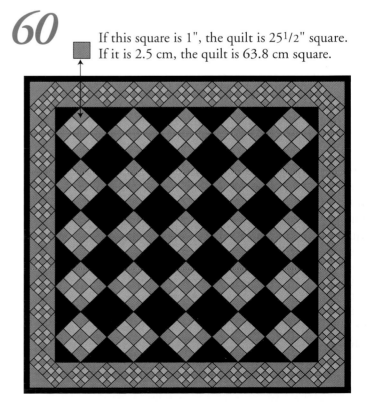

The Secret of the Setting Triangles

In a quilt with a diagonal set, the blocks are set on point, rather than parallel to the sides of the quilt. These diagonal rows create the need for half squares of setting triangles at each end.

Cutting these triangles can be tricky, unless you know the secret. It's no secret that two right triangles can be made by cutting a square in half diagonally. However, when the squares are fabric and they have been cut on grain, the hypotenuse, or longest edge, of the new triangles would be a perfect bias and very stretchy. When triangles like that are added to the end of a row, that stretchy edge is on the outside of the quilt, an arrangement that is difficult at best, disastrous at worst.

It is obvious that setting triangles with the hypotenuse, or longest side, on the straight grain are preferred. How to do that is the Secret of the Setting Triangles. From a square of fabric that is larger than the block size, cut on both diagonals to yield four setting triangles, **Diagram A**.

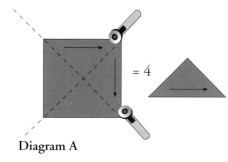

Diagram A

To determine the size of the square, measure the diagonal of the finished size unit block, and add 1 1/4 inches **Diagram B**. This is the size square to quarter for perfect-fit, no-mistakes-allowed setting triangles. I prefer to add 1 1/2 to 2 1/2 inches to the diagonal measurement of the block. That size square will yield slightly larger setting triangles, which allow the blocks to float inside the borders, **Diagram C**.

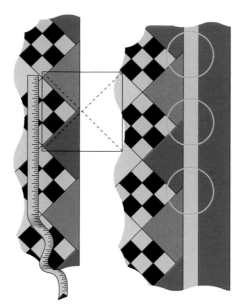

Diagram B   Diagram C

The more you add to the square, the more the quilt blocks float. Floating is good insurance against nipping off the corners of the quilt blocks when adding the borders, which will happen if the setting triangles don't fit perfectly, **Diagram D**. A narrow float actually makes your piecing look more crisp because you can see the corner points of the quilt blocks. A wide float can serve as a narrow first border. Excess can be trimmed away later if you decide you don't want a floating set.

Diagram D

Warning: The square method for cutting setting triangles shown in **Diagram A** is the easiest, but it doesn't always work with directional fabric. Also, the grain on half of the resulting triangles is on the straight lengthwise grain, and half is on straight crosswise grain. As discussed on page 18, the crosswise grain has more stretch than the lengthwise.

First, let's talk about directional fabric. We have already warned about the use of directional or one-way designs in the Nine Patch. Here we go again. You might want the design running one way on the top and bottom of the quilt, and the other way in the setting triangles on the sides. If so, you could use the square method, but remember, the number you need of each is often uneven, and there will be waste.

However, if the design is something like trees, or houses, or horses, it is unlikely that you will want half of them laying on their sides, **Diagram E**.

Second, grainline perfectionists might not be satisfied with different

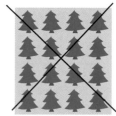

Diagram E

grain on the setting triangles. To completely minimize stretch on the outside edge of the quilt, cut the setting triangles from strips cut on the lengthwise grain, as described on the next page.

The Other Secret

At some time, you may need to know the other way to cut setting triangles. This strip technique involves cutting strips on the lengthwise grain, unless a directional fabric design demands the crosswise grain, and then cutting triangles from the strips.

How wide is the strip? Calculate the width by dividing the finished size of the block by 1.41. Add $5/8$-inch for triangles with no float, or add $7/8$ to $1 1/2$ inches for float. Remember, the more you add, the greater the float. (This chart lists the measurements for the most common Nine Patch block sizes.)

Strip Widths for Setting Triangles When Using the Strip Method	
Most Common Finished Sizes of Nine Patch Blocks	Strip Width with No Float*
3"	2$3/4$"
4$1/2$"	3$3/4$"
6"	4$7/8$"
7$1/2$"	6$1/16$"
9"	7"

* Add $1/2$ inch to 1 inch additional width to strips for float.

After cutting strips, use a ruler with a 45-degree angle line to cut away the end, **Diagram F**. Save this piece. Rotate the ruler. Line up the edge exactly on the corner and any inch mark line with the just-cut edge, **Diagram G**. Cut and create a perfect setting triangle.

Rotate ruler again, line up an inch mark on the most recently cut edge and the edge of the ruler with the corner, **Diagram H**. Cut. Check and make sure your triangles match and are the correct size, then continue.

Diagram F

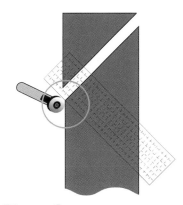

Diagram G

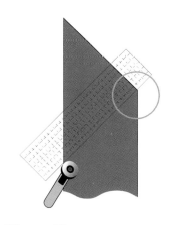

Diagram H

Cutting the Corner Triangles

When cutting the right triangles for the corners, the desired grainline is just the opposite of the setting triangles. The hypotenuse should be on the bias and the legs on the straight grain. Four corner triangles can be cut from two squares that are the same size as the master block. Cut each square in half diagonally to yield triangles with the legs on the straight grain, **Diagram I**.

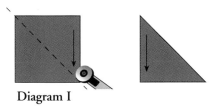

Diagram I

These triangles will be oversized enough to match floating setting triangles Don't panic if they don't match perfectly. Excess fabric can be trimmed away later.

If you have used the strip method, the first triangles cut away from the end of the strip are usually the correct size for the corner triangles, and they are the correct grain. If you have added an unusually large amount of float, you may need to cut larger corner triangles.

The Moral of the Story

Always analyze your right triangles carefully. If you want the hypotenuse to be on straight grain, quarter a square diagonally. If you want the hypotenuse of all the triangles on the straight lengthwise grain, cut the triangles from strips cut on the lengthwise grain.

If you want the legs or short sides to be on the straight grain, halve a square diagonally.

61 1890s Nine Patch

The finished size of the new quilt, shown on the wall, is 47" x 57" (117.5 cm x 142.5 cm) square. The finished size of the Nine Patch block is 3" (7.5 cm).

The finished size of the antique quilt, shown on the quilt rack, is 40" x 45 1/2" (100 cm x 113.8 cm). The finished size of that Nine Patch block is 2 5/8" (6.6 cm).

Scrap Nine Patch blocks make wonderful quilts. As you will see by looking closely at Quilts 61 and 62 above, nearly any fabric can be used in the Nine Patch units and then be easily "tamed" by using a consistent fabric in the alternate blocks. The most common, and I think most attractive, combinations match dark scraps in the five position of the 5/4 Nine Patch with light alternate blocks and vice versa. This eliminates the possibility for an embedded chain look and creates an emphasis on the scrap look.

On pages 28 and 29, we discussed how enlarging a Nine Patch block by 1/4 inch results in bigger blocks and, often, the elimination of one row, while still making a quilt the same size. That is exactly the case with these two quilts–but with an even smaller increase in size! The antique quilt is based on a square that is 7/8-inch finished. The new quilt is based on 1-inch squares. I made 63 blocks, instead of 80, added a float allowance and slightly larger border; the finished quilt is actually larger than the old.

Make Scrap Blocks Using Strip Techniques

When I was studying the antique crib quilt, it became clear that many of the blocks were repeated three times. That is enough to justify cutting strips. To get matching Nine Patch blocks, the strips need to be six times as long as they are wide for the fabrics in Rows 1 and 3 and three times as long as wide for Row 2. Make 63.

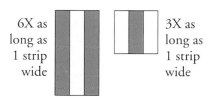

6X as long as 1 strip wide

3X as long as 1 strip wide

For Three Nine Patch Blocks Cut Fabric for Alternate Squares and Chain Piece

Confirm the size of your Nine Patch blocks before cutting the strips for the alternate blocks. Cut strips as wide as the Nine Patch blocks. The total length of the strips should be 48 times the size of the Nine Patch. (In my quilt with 3-inch finished Nine Patch blocks, five strips cut 3 1/2 inches wide by 36 inches long would be just fine.)

Chain piece 48 of the Nine Patch blocks to the strips of alternate-block fabric. Press the strip away from the

Nine Patch blocks. The seam allowance should be under the long strip.

Now use your rotary cutter, ruler and mat to cut apart. Put one of the horizontal ruler lines on the seam line and check accuracy. Cut background strip to create squares. Repeat on other side of block, if necessary, and repeat with each block.

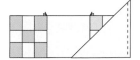

Cut Setting Triangles and Lay Out Quilt

Follow the instructions on pages 78 and 79 to cut 28 setting triangles. Arrange the 48 pairs and the leftover Nine Patch blocks into diagonal rows. Much of the charm of the antique quilt is due to the random fashion in which the blocks are arranged. To achieve that authentic look, do not over-plan the placement of the blocks.

Piecing the Diagonal Rows

1. The easiest and least confusing way to join the diagonal rows is to start by joining the Nine Patch/alternate block combinations within each row.

2. The next step is to sew the setting triangles in the appropriate positions. Each diagonal row will begin and end with one of the 28 setting triangles. (The four triangles that make up the four corners of the quilt are not added until the border has been attached.) Line up the right angle of the setting triangle with a corner of the Nine Patch block so that the hypotenuse (longest edge) will become the outside edge of the quilt. The tips of the triangles will extend beyond the patchwork in both directions. Stitch.

Press seams toward the triangles.

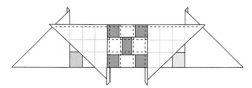

3. When each diagonal row has been completed, the rows can be stitched to one another following your layout plan. Begin in the upper left corner with the single Nine Patch in Row 1 and, with right sides of fabric together, sew it to Row 2.

Row 3 is then joined to Row 2, and so on, until all the diagonal rows have been sewn together.

Note: When joining the rows, the extending tips of the triangles will need to be sewn one over the other, thus creating the effect of floating triangles. Trim off the stitched-across triangle tips and excess seam allowances before layering the quilt top for finishing.

To complete the quilt top, narrow white and pink strips were sewn to each corner, then pink strips on all four sides. Then the corner triangles were added and, finally, white borders.

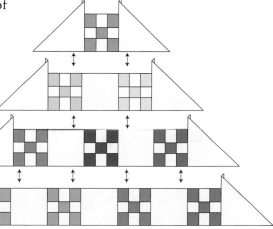

62 1890s Nine Patch in Reverse

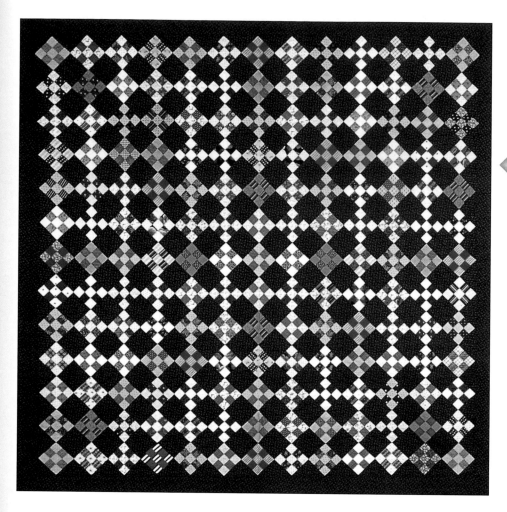

The finished size of this quilt is 61¹/₂" (153.75 cm) square.
The finished size of the Nine Patch block is 3" (7.5 cm).

Compare this quilt to 1890s Nine Patch, Quilt 61. In this quilt, the values
are reversed. Dark alternate blocks replace light, and light fabrics are used in
the five position of the Nine Patch blocks.

Tip
Calculating Sizes of Diagonal Set Quilts

When Nine Patch quilts are straight
set, figuring the size is usually very
straightforward. All you need to know
is the size of the square and how many
there are in each direction.

With diagonal set quilts, there is
another step: determining the diagonal dimension of the blocks. Just multiply the size of the block by 1.41; a
small calculator is very handy for this
task. Use this number to calculate the
size of the patchwork. Don't forget to
add the dimension of the borders.

This chart includes the diagonal size
of the most common Nine Patch
block sizes. Calculate other sizes.

Finished Block Size		Diagonal Size
3"	=	4¹/₄"-
4¹/₂"	=	6³/₈"-
6"	=	8¹/₂"-
7¹/₂"	=	10⁵/₈"-
9"	=	12⁵/₈"+

Note: + or - means less than
¹/₁₆-inch over or under the
size given.

63 Over the Rainbow

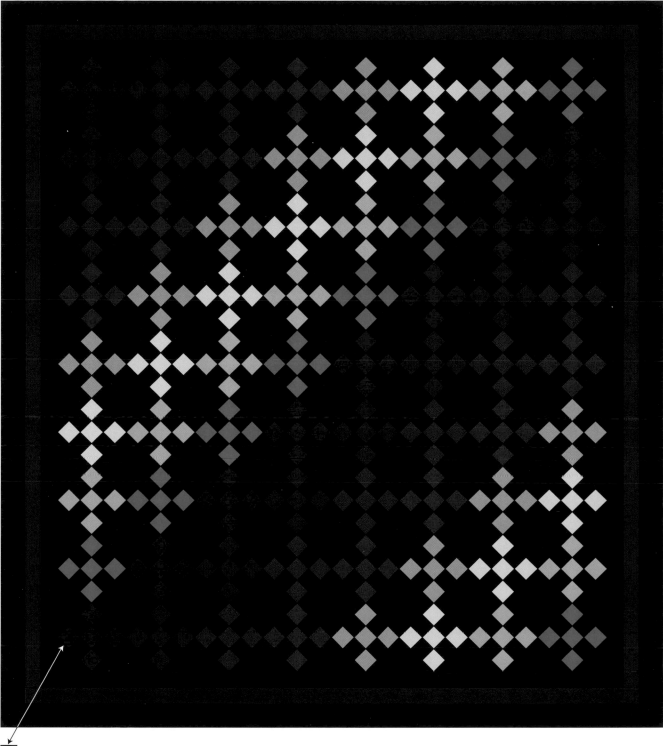

If this square is 1", the finished size is 42¹/4" x 46¹/2".
If this square is 2.5 cm, the finished size is 105.6 cm x 116.3 cm.

Instead of scraps in the Nine Patch units, consider very organized patterns of color like Over the Rainbow. Select eight colors in a rainbow range. Make nine Nine Patches of each color with the color in the five position and the fabric you selected for the alternate blocks in the four position. Cut setting triangles and corner triangles following guidelines on pages 78 and 79.

64 Double Nine Patch Chain

If this square is 1", the finished size is 56³/4" x 69¹/2".
If this square is 2.5 cm, the finished size is 141.9 cm x 173.8 cm.

Turn the Double Nine Patch on point and you create a more elaborate chain than the Nine Patch Chain on page 76. You can still create an embedded look, as shown on page 76. Use the same fabric in the large alternating blocks as is used in the four position of the Double Nine Patch blocks. The resulting open space invites beautiful quilting.

Tip · Shortcut for Calculating Different Sizes

All of the quilts have dimensions based on the smallest square being one inch. To determine a new size, simply multiply those dimensions by alternate larger or smaller size squares.

Example: The 1-inch dimension of the Double Nine Patch quilt is 56³/4" x 69¹/2". If the smallest square was 1¹/4 inch instead of 1 inch, the quilt would be 56.75" times 1.25" by 69.5" times 1.25", or approximately 71" by 87".

Likewise, a 1¹/2" smallest square would be 56.75" times 1.5" by 69.5" times 1.5", or approximately 85" by 104", a great queen/double quilt size.

For metric, multiply the finished 1-inch dimensions by the new metric sizes; you will be converting to metric and calculating new sizes at the same time.

The Double Nine Patch Chain Gang

64b

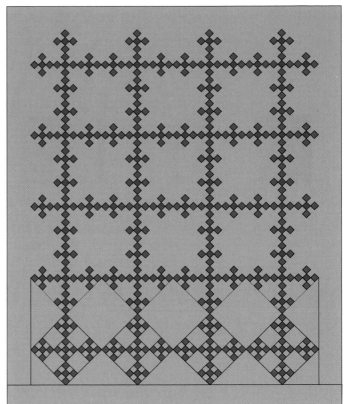

64a

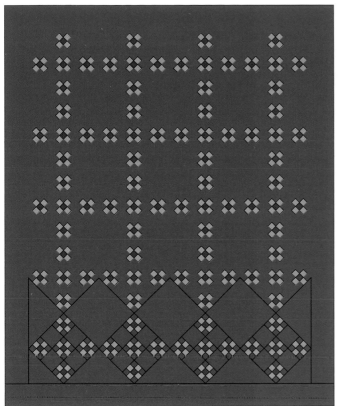

64c

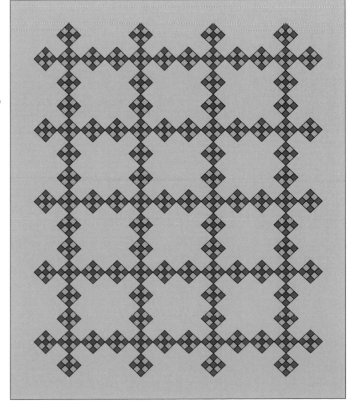

All of the quilts on this page are made the same way; their differences are perceptual. The Nine Patch blocks are identical. However, in Quilt 64a, the background matches the darkest value in the Double Nine Patch blocks, which brightens the lighter units in the quilt. In Quilt 64b, the background matches the lightest value in the blocks and brings out the dark corners of the Nine Patch blocks. In 64c, the medium value background sets off both the light and dark smaller squares.

65 Nine Patch Trellis

If this square is 1", the finished size is $56^{3}/4$" x $69^{1}/2$".
If this square is 2.5 cm, the finished size is 141.9 cm x 173.8 cm.

If the square is $1^{1}/2$", the quilt is 85" x 104", a great queen/double size. Add another vertical row of double Nine patch blocks for a king size, or 104" square, quilt.

65a

65b

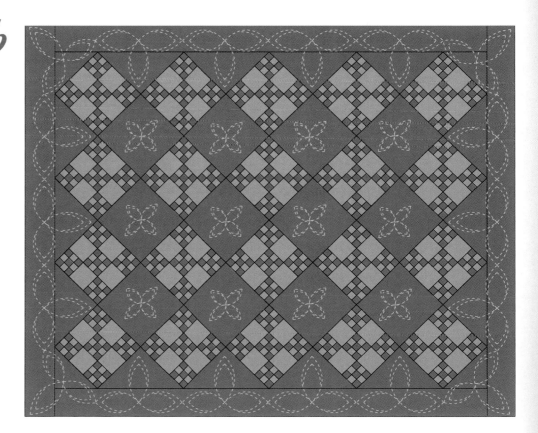

In Quilt 65, the floral border matches the setting triangles. Large plain alternate blocks match the alternate blocks in the Double Nine Patches.

Create a wonderful area for a quilting design by replacing large alternate blocks with a contrasting color, as we did in Quilt 65a.

Want more quilting area? Use the plan for Quilt 65b–eliminate the floral fabric and quilt in all the plain areas. As a bonus, the Nine Patch blocks become more visible.

66 Amish Magic Nine Patch

The finished size of this quilt is 19¼" (48.1 cm) square.
The finished size of the Nine Patch block is 3" (7.5 cm).

With this quilt, the designs move to continuous Nine Patch blocks in a diagonal set. Endless designs can be created by changing colors. The next few pages will showcase some beautiful quilts that are also efficiently made with strip techniques.

What Makes the Magic Nine Patch "Magic"?
Most magic is an illusion, often a sleight of hand that makes the observer believe something has happened, when, in fact, it has not.

To find the magic in the Magic Nine Patch, look at the photo of the Amish Magic Nine Patch above. Most people see the bright blue grid of squares and the squares they contain and think that is the quilt block. This unit is, in fact, a popular quilt block pattern called an Album or Friendship block, which contains

25 pieces: 13 squares on point, eight setting triangles and four corner triangles:

Put nine of those Album blocks together in three rows of three.

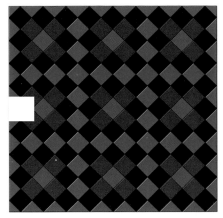

Like magic, the setting and corner triangles from the individual blocks touch and become squares. However, the outside edge seems incomplete.

Look closely and you can see that the new design is actually created by alternating these two different Nine Patch combinations in a diagonal set.

Block A   **Block B**

There is a Trick
Always think of the two blocks as Block A and Block B. Block A is usually made in the typical high contrast five/four arrangement. In the Amish Magic Nine Patch, that would be the royal blue (five) and black (four). The fabric in the five position of Block A connects and creates the chain of color in both directions across the quilt. Block B is made in a 4/4/1 combination. The corner four fabrics in Block B must match the fabric in the four position of Block A. When the blocks are put together, these squares create the concentric frame of eight squares around the center pieces of Block B. The other four matching squares in Block B must contrast strongly with the first four squares as well as the center square.

With this trick, what looks difficult is really quite simple. Extra Nine Patch blocks continue the pattern all the way to the border, and when trimmed, appear to be pieced setting and corner triangles.

Can Nine Patch Blocks Be Cut in Half to Make Setting Triangles?
Not unless you are willing to sacrifice points on the outside edge of the quilt. Typically, you want more than half a Nine Patch, anyway.

To get complete royal blue squares on the edge of the Amish Magic Patch required parts of 16 blue and black Nine Patch blocks while only nine red, black and green blocks are used in the quilt interior.

Twelve individual setting triangles are cut for these positions and sewn to the ends of each row before assembly. →

After the rows were assembled, the quilt interior was trimmed 1/4-inch beyond the corner of the royal blue squares.

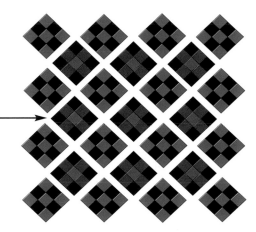

Setting triangles

Other Edge Treatments
If the square in a Nine Patch is larger than two inches, especially for a bed quilt, I would make the effort to cut and piece setting triangles with the hypotenuse on straight grain.

If you don't do special cutting on larger pieces, handle the pieces very carefully and add a border immedi-

ately. If the border is not ready to add, stay-stitch the outside edge of the quilt! A stay-stitch is a regular machine stitch (10-12 stitches per inch) a scant 1/4-inch from the edge.

67 Baby Magic Nine Patch

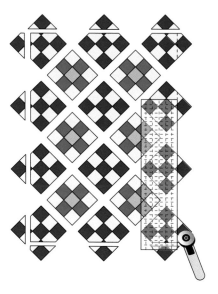

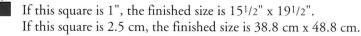

If this square is 1", the finished size is 15$\frac{1}{2}$" x 19$\frac{1}{2}$".
If this square is 2.5 cm, the finished size is 38.8 cm x 48.8 cm.

Need a super quick baby quilt? Make larger blocks from bright juvenile prints with this layout and 3-inch (7.5 cm) cut strips.

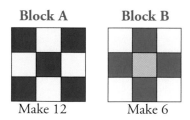

Block A

Make 12

Block B

Make 6

Trim the blocks as shown. Be sure to position the ruler $\frac{1}{4}$-inch beyond the point of the square to create the $\frac{1}{4}$-inch seam allowance.

Cut 10 individual setting triangles to complete the rows. Cut three 6-inch squares and cut diagonally twice (see page 78). There will be some float allowance and two extra triangles.

Assemble the blocks and setting triangles into rows and finish the quilt interior as usual. Trim away excess and add 7 inches of borders for a quilt that finishes approximately 43$\frac{3}{4}$" x 56$\frac{1}{2}$" or 109.4 cm x 141.3 cm.

Create Your Own Diagonal Set Design

Photocopy the grid below and use colored pencils, markers or crayons to design your own diagonal set Nine Patch quilt.

68 Lavender Blue Dilly Dilly

The finished size of the quilt in the photograph on the opposite page is 78" x 98" (195 cm x 245 cm) square.

The finished size of the Nine Patch block is 7$\frac{1}{2}$" (18.8 cm).

The Magic Nine Patch adventure continues. Look at Block A. Usually, Block A is a typical high contrast 5/4 arrangement, but here we are looking at 5/2/2.

Block A

Make 24

Block B

Make 18

Block C

Make 17

Once again, the fabric in the five position of Block A will form the continuous lines of color in both directions of the quilt.

In the two previous Magic Nine Patch quilts, the four corners of Block B matched the fabric in the four position of Block A. In this quilt, the four corners of Block B match two squares of Block A and

the four corners of Block C match the other two squares in the 5/2/2 arrangement of Block A.

Every other diagonal row alternates. The first row has Block B, while the next row has Blocks A and Blocks C. The third row includes Blocks A and Block B, et cetera. Block A is rotated appropriately to develop this new pattern.

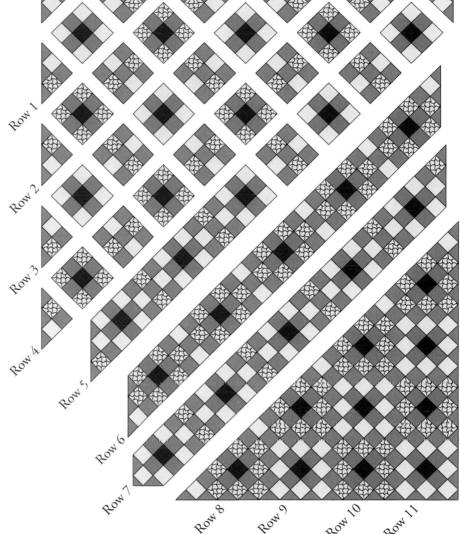

Because the strips for this size quilt are cut 3 inches wide and because it is a bed quilt that can expect heavy use, I recommend cutting separate small setting triangles for pieced setting triangles and corners.

Follow the guidelines on pages 78 and 79 for cutting.

Remember the Rule of Matching Corners
If you want to change the size or shape of this quilt, it will be much more attractive if you add or subtract two rows at a time. That will ensure that the colors in the corners match.

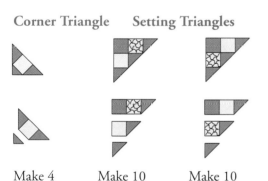

Corner Triangle   **Setting Triangles**

Make 4   Make 10   Make 10

Lavender Blue Dilly Dilly makes a lovely queen/double size quilt.

69 Album Nine Patch

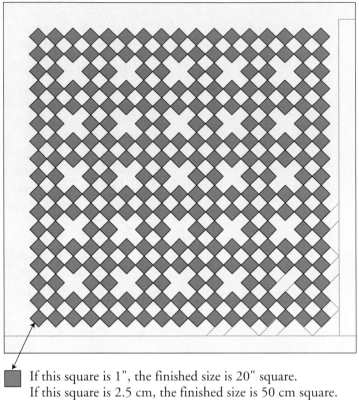

If this square is 1", the finished size is 20" square.
If this square is 2.5 cm, the finished size is 50 cm square.

Block B

Make 25

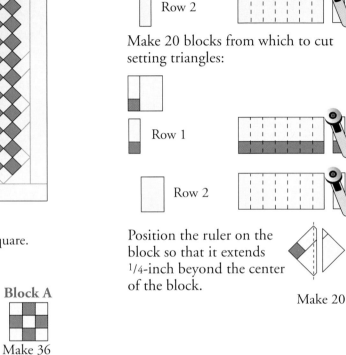

Rows 1

Row 2

Make 20 blocks from which to cut setting triangles:

Row 1

Row 2

Position the ruler on the block so that it extends 1/4-inch beyond the center of the block.

Make 20

Block A

Make 36

One of the wonderful things about strip technique quilts is that all you need to design them is graph paper and colored pencils. When you start coloring in the squares, remember to play with omission as a design technique.

The Album Nine Patch introduces a very simple arrangement we have not used previously in a Nine Patch block. The block has five squares of one color and four of another, but not in the typical checkerboard arrangement.

The quilt could be called a variation of a Magic Nine Patch because the fabric in the four corners of Block B matches the four fabric in the traditional 5/4 checkerboard arrangement of Block A.

Limit yourself to two colors and the repeat will be even more mystifying to your friends. An entire Nine Patch is used in each corner to continue the pattern of a double row of squares. Look at Gold Nine on page 96, to see this design with four colors.

69a Miniature Album Nine

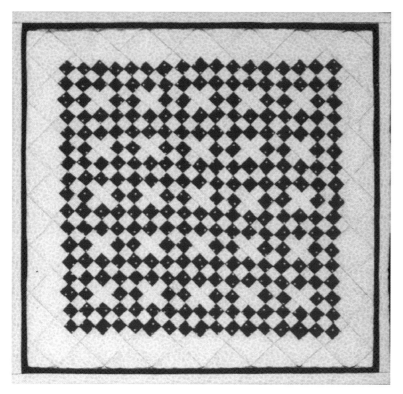

The finished size of this quilt is 15" (37.5 cm) square.
The finished size of the Nine Patch block is 1¹/2" (3.8 cm).

Tip *Adding a Flap*

The narrow red flap adds just the right accent on the outer edge. To make a flap, cut a strip ⁷/8" to 1" wide on the straight grain. Fold in half wrong sides together and press. Align the long raw edge with the edge of one side of the quilt and stitch in place. Trim excess and repeat on the opposite side. Repeat on the other two sides. Bind the quilt as usual. Don't try to stitch the flap in place as you add the binding. The resulting corners are a mess.

Block A

Make 36

Block B

Make 25

The miniature quilt in the photo has the same number of blocks as Album Nine Patch, but they are made from 1-inch cut strips. Each square is ¹/2-inch finished.

There are several differences in how these two quilts were made, although either quilt could be made using any of these techniques.

Here, small red squares were appliqued to larger ecru squares to complete the final row of chained squares. Setting triangles were cut slightly larger than needed to allow extra float allowance.

Setting Blocks

Make 20

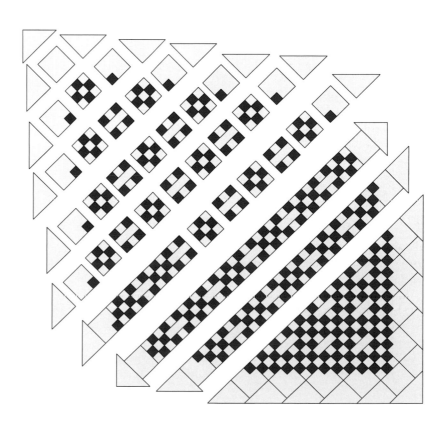

70 Gold Nine

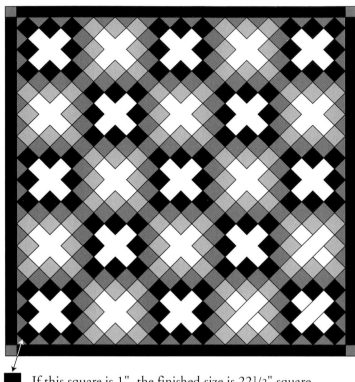

 If this square is 1", the finished size is 22¹/₂" square.
If this square is 2.5 cm, the finished size is 56.3 cm square.

Nine Patch Block 1
Make 13

Nine Patch Block 2
Make 36

Nine Patch Block 3
Make 12

Gold Nine is Album Nine Patch with two more colors. The medium value creates the chain in this design, leaving room for more dramatic results with the dark and light fabrics.

Assemble the diagonal rows. Trim away excess, but leave a ¹/₄-inch seam allowance.

71 Nine Patch Friends

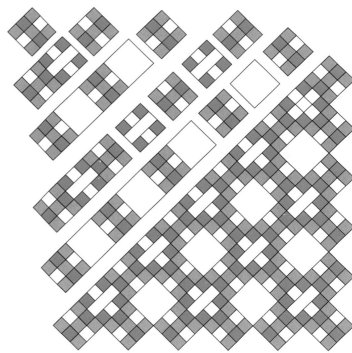

When you omit a Nine Patch and replace it with a plain alternate block, it becomes Nine Patch Friends, which is a lot like Fenced in Chickens, page 52, turned on point.

The alternate empty squares would be perfect for collecting signatures or inking collected sayings.

Design Your Own

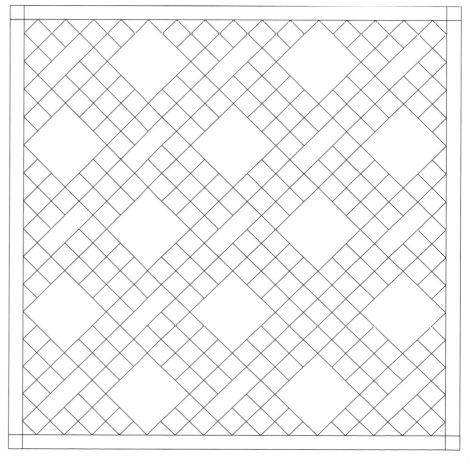

72 Nine Patch & Singleton

The idea for Nine Patch and Single-ton came about as I was doodling on diagonal graph paper. I had been thinking about creating a border with Nine Patch blocks chained together with a single square. As I doodled, I realized that a single small square could be part of a Nine Patch. Look at the column of blocks to see the progressive result of asking, "What if…?"

1. The Nine Patch and Singleton are shown on a grid, set on point.

2. Using a third fabric in the five position of the Nine Patch and the background of Singleton clearly defines the blocks.

3. Putting a third fabric in the setting triangle is another way to define the blocks.

4. Make the setting triangles and the background of the Singleton and Nine Patch blocks match, and the patchwork will appear embedded.

In the examples shown, the Singleton matches the Nine Patch. If you change the color of the Singleton, the number of combinations to consider doubles.

5. The embedded look was very appealing to me and I wanted to see what two rows staggered would look like.

6. Then I colored the centers of the Singleton blocks.

That looked good, so I wanted to look at the staggered rows in an all-over design. On graph paper, the overall pattern filled the quilt center. Then it was surrounded by an empty section and then a double border. The empty section is made of squares the same size as the Nine Patch blocks.

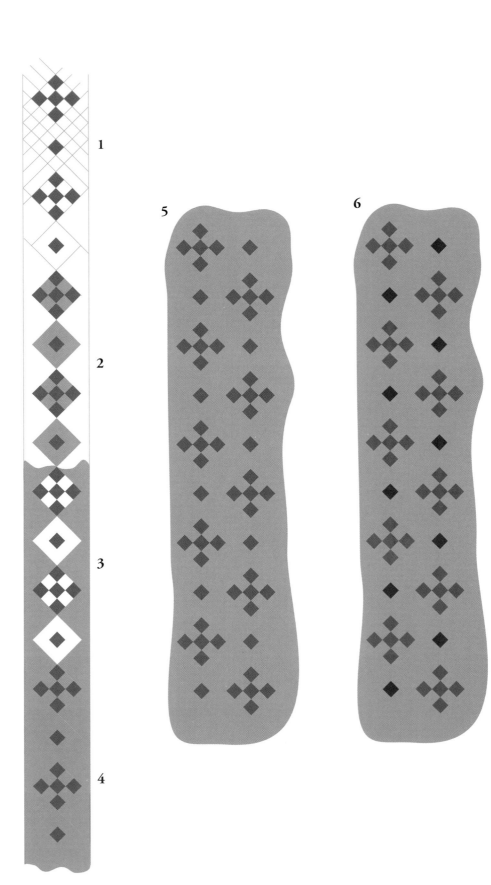

The finished size of this quilt is 40" x 48¹/2" (100 cm x 121.3 cm). The finished size of the Nine Patch block is 3" (7.5 cm).

Singleton Block

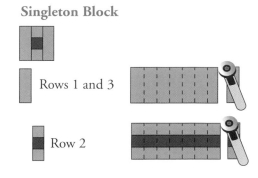

Rows 1 and 3

Row 2

Tip *Perfect Borders*

One way to get perfectly fitting borders is to design them into the patchwork plan.

Omission is actually used twice in designing this quilt, once to create the Singleton block and once to create the borders. This quilt really has almost three borders:

1. The wide strip of matching background fabric.

2. The Nine Patch and Singleton corners.

3. The contrasting Sawtooth edge.

The key to ease of construction is that all of the components are made with the same size unit block.

Cutting the background fabric in unit block squares and sewing them back together may seem strange, but it is easy to do and creates perfect lines for machine quilting in the ditch.

73 Atlanta Commons

If this square is 1", the finished size is $46^1/2$" x $59^1/4$".
If this square is 2.5 cm, the finished size is 116.3 cm x 148.1 cm.

This well-planned quilt is made of touching Nine Patch blocks, colored as a single design. Look back at Linked Scrappy Nines, Quilt 12, on page 31 to see the same layout in a straight set.

Making Your Own
Atlanta Commons

One of the wonderful things about strip techniques is the versatility of size. This quilt would make a beautiful wall hanging with 3/4" or 1-inch (1.9 cm or 2.5 cm) finished squares in the Nine Patch. But, enlarge the finished square to 1³/4" (4.4 cm) and you'll have a wonderful queen/ double quilt, at least 80¹/2" x 102³/4" (201.3 cm x 256.9 cm), depending on border widths. Refer to the chart on page 14 to estimate the yardage needed for each block.

		# of Nine Patch Blocks		# of Squares Per Block		Total # of Squares This Color
Used in every block	My consistent fabric	196	x	4	=	784
My fabric swatch		38	x	5	=	190
My fabric swatch		34	x	5	=	170
My fabric swatch		30	x	5	=	150
My fabric swatch		26	x	5	=	130
My fabric swatch		22	x	5	=	110
My fabric swatch		18	x	5	=	90
My fabric swatch		14	x	5	=	70
My fabric swatch		10	x	5	=	50
My fabric swatch		4	x	5	=	20

74 Indian Blanket

If this square is 1", the finished size is 38" x 46½".
If this square is 2.5 cm, the finished size is 95 cm x 116.3 cm.

What makes this quilt stand out from the other Nine Patch and alternate block designs is that it, like Atlanta Commons, was colored as one unit.

Dazzling rectangles of concentric color conceal the simplicity of the quilt.

The fabric for the plain alternate blocks should be slightly lighter than the Nine Patch companion blocks.

75 Indian Village

Look at the Indian Blanket layout. Replace two black corners on each Nine Patch block with a neutral fabric. Suddenly the small black squares become the more obvious concentric rectangles.

Don't forget that each concentric rectangle requires four corner blocks.

Nine Patch Blocks

Rows 1 and 3

Row 2

Corner Blocks

Rows 1 and 3

Row 2

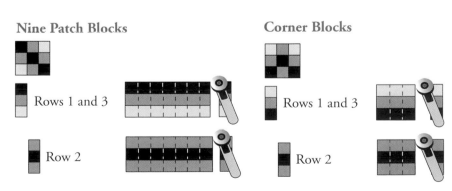

76 Garden Variety

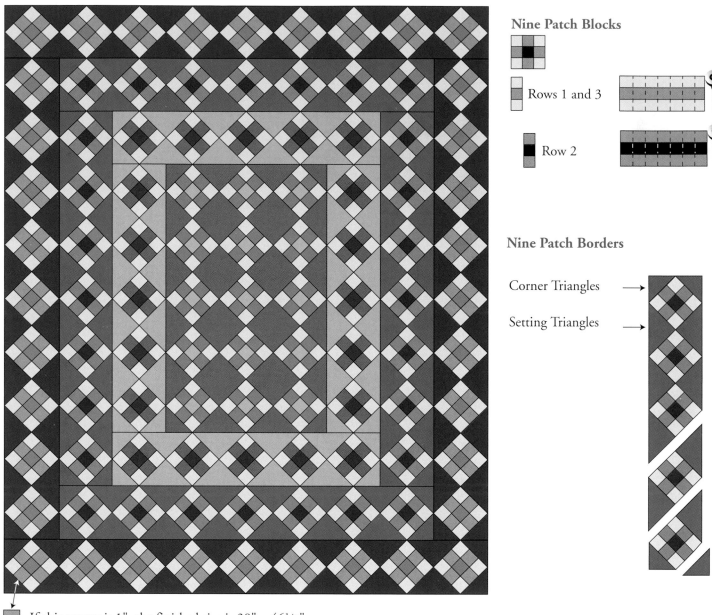

Nine Patch Blocks

Rows 1 and 3

Row 2

Nine Patch Borders

Corner Triangles →

Setting Triangles →

If this square is 1", the finished size is 38" x 46¹/₂".
If this square is 2.5 cm, the finished size is 95 cm x 116.3 cm.

In Garden Variety, half-square triangles replace alternate squares. This creates even more rigid rectangles of color. The Nine Patch blocks are colored in the 4/4/1 arrangement.

Turning the Corners
You may be wondering how to piece the sections where the color turns a corner. The easiest way is to treat each "frame" of color like a border.

Make four separate sections for each border. In this quilt layout, each border has four equal sections. Cut four corner triangles for each section and the appropriate number of setting triangles. See pages 78 and 79 for more cutting information.

77 A Smaller Garden

In A Smaller Garden, there is one less frame of Nine Patch blocks and a thin border that matches the final row of triangles and creates a great sawtooth edge.

Eliminating the frame saves 400 pieces of patchwork. No matter how fast you are, if you can eliminate pieces without sacrificing design, you can make more quilts, faster.

If this square is 1", the finished size is 33 1/4" x 38".
If this square is 2.5 cm, the finished size is 83.1 cm x 95 cm.

78 City Garden

City Garden has even less patchwork, but still creates the same design feeling.

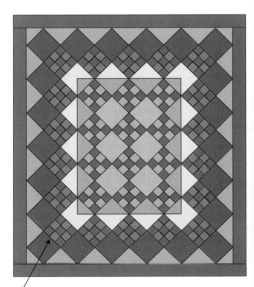

If this square is 1", the finished size is 29 5/8" x 33 7/8".

If this square is 2.5 cm, the finished size is 74.1 cm x 84.7 cm.

Mirror Tricks

There are endless possibilities for this family of quilts. Study the combinations in these rows for more arrangements similar to Garden Variety and Indian Village.

If you have one of the folding mirrors, place it at a 90-degree angle at the center of each quadrant to see a complete picture of each possibility shown.

79 Strippy Nine Patch

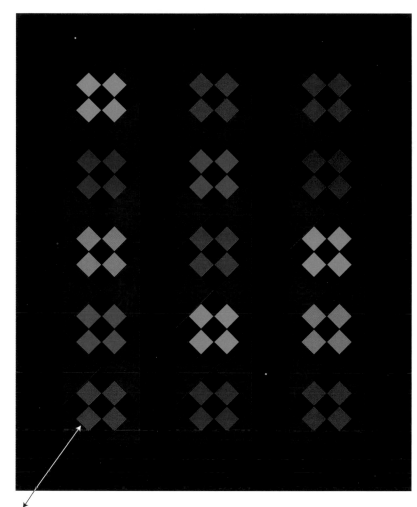

Arrangement for assembly of one row
Make 3

Corner Triangles ⟶

Setting Triangles ⟶

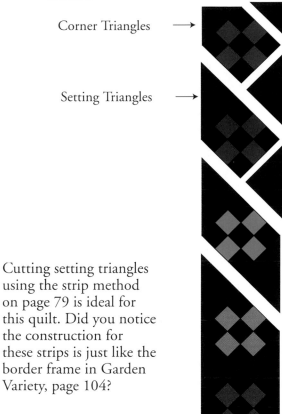

Cutting setting triangles using the strip method on page 79 is ideal for this quilt. Did you notice the construction for these strips is just like the border frame in Garden Variety, page 104?

If this square is 1", the finished size is 22½" x 26¾".
If this square is 2.5 cm, the finished size is 56.3 cm x 66.9 cm.

80 Strippy Nine Patch

Rotate the color into the five position of the classic 5/4 arrangement and the Nine Patch blocks in the strippy arrangement become chained. You may also like extra color in the dividing strip.

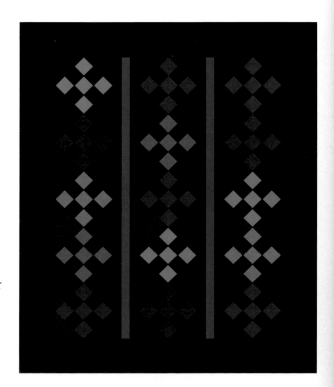

81 Secret Nine Patch

This design has a secret. It's a Nine Patch in a Nine Patch. Make the 32 Secret Nine Patch blocks and finish the interior section with large setting triangles. The wonderful border is a strip of Nine Patch blocks combined with appropriate setting triangles. It is completed with a plain border.

Block A **Block B**

Note that the small Nine Patch blocks in the centers of Blocks A and B match in a 4/4/1 arrangement. The small blocks in the border also match each other but are the classic 5/4 arrangement with dark corners.

☐ If this square is 1", the finished size is $67^5/8$" x $80^3/8$".
If this square is 2.5 cm, the finished size is 169.1 cm x 200.1 cm.

82 009 Patch

With a simple manipulation of values and elimination of the last plain border, the 009 Nine Patch takes on a completely different look and a slightly smaller size.

83 Main Streets

 If this square is 1", the finished size is 25¼" x 29½".
If this square is 2.5 cm, the finished size is 63.1 cm x 73.8 cm.

Fence Rail Blocks

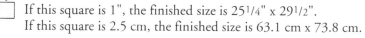

Corner Triangles

Setting Triangles

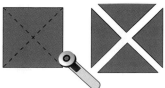

Once more, Fence Rail and Nine Patch block are united, but this time they are on point. Don't forget to rotate the Fence Rail block in every other row.

Design Your Own

84 Framed Nine Patch on Point

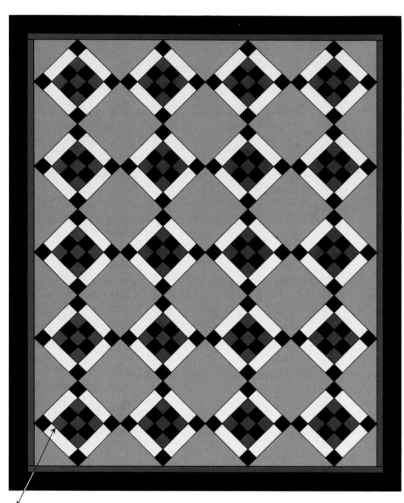

85 Frame Game

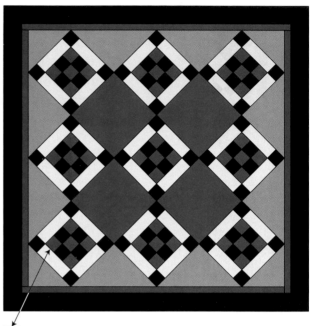

If this square is 1", the finished size is $25^1/_2$" square.

If this square is 2.5 cm, the finished size is 63.7 cm square.

If this square is 1", the finished size is $32^1/_2$" x $39^1/_2$".
If this square is 2.5 cm, the finished size is 81.3 cm x 98.7 cm.

86 Framed and Chained

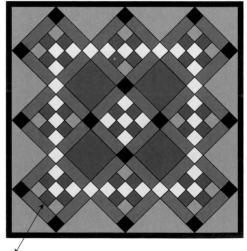

Make complete Framed Nine Patch blocks and then cut plain alternate squares the same size. Cut appropriate setting and corner triangles. Assemble using the typical diagonal rows.

When corners of the Framed Nine Patch blocks overlap, as they do in Framed and chained, the "frames" are treated like separate diagonal rows of sashing.

If this square is 1", the finished size is $18^1/_2$" square.

If this square is 2.5 cm, the finished size is 46.3 cm square.

Nine Patch Partners

In the first two quilt sections, the shapes used in the quilts were limited to squares and strips plus setting triangles and corner triangles when the quilts were set on point. This maximized the flexibility of size with strip techniques.

This section features Nine Patch blocks as partners with other shapes in creating beautiful quilts. The emphasis is on triangles because with just a little math, they can be cut without patterns. There are a few other shapes, and a few of the quilts require patterns, which are included, but limit the sizes of the quilts.

When you look through your favorite books and periodicals, turn on your Nine Patch alert system and you will find even more quilts where the Nine Patch is a key component.

87 Nine Patch Furrows

Half-square Triangles

Cut strips.

Cut strips into squares.

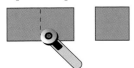

Cut squares into triangles.

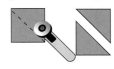

Chain piece triangles into half-square triangle units.

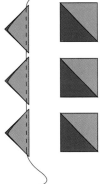

If this square is 1", the finished size is 35" x 41".
If this square is 2.5 cm, the finished size is 87.5 cm x 102.5 cm.

Tip

Make Sewing Easier

Before cutting, place the two fabrics for the half-square triangle units right sides together. Cut strips. Do not separate the strips. Cut the squares, then the triangles. The triangle pairs will be perfectly positioned for chain piecing. It not only saves time, but also increases accuracy.

Nine Patch Furrows would be particularly nice as a bed-size quilt. One-way diagonal lines give a bed quilt a contemporary feeling so this might be a particularly good choice if you want a contemporary look.

Cut strips for the Nine Patch $2^3/4$ inches (6.9 cm) wide and the finished block will be $6^3/4$ inches (16.9 cm). Using the layout shown, the quilt will be $79^3/4$" x $93^1/4$" (199.4 cm x 233.1 cm).

Make 50 Nine Patch blocks. They are shown all alike here and flanked with country colors. For a contemporary quilt, think about assorted black and white prints for the Nine Patch

blocks and clear bright colors for the triangles.

Cutting Half-square Triangles
Next, you will need to make what are commonly called half-square triangles. Of course, it isn't triangles that you want; you want squares made from two half-square triangles. Plus, you're picky, you want the new squares to be the same size as the Nine Patch blocks you have just made! If you were making a crib quilt with 3-inch Nine Patch blocks, I would recommend using the appropriate half-square triangle in Set A of From Marti Michell Perfect Patchwork Templates to quick cut the triangle pairs.

Regardless of the availability of some templates, you want the flexibility of making the Nine Patch blocks any size. That is why you want to learn the rule for cutting half-square triangles without a pattern. It isn't hard. It is sometimes awkward. This is one of those times.

Let's talk about 3-inch squares first. We know that a 3-inch finished square will be $3\frac{1}{2}$ inches before it is sewn. It would be easy to jump to the conclusion that you should cut $3\frac{1}{2}$-inch squares in half diagonally, but that size isn't big enough to include the $\frac{1}{4}$-inch seam allowance on the hypotenuse of the triangle.

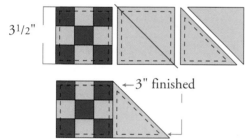

This triangle is too small.

A New Magic Number
So, how big should your squares be? You can find out if you draw the finished size right triangle, and then add a $\frac{1}{4}$-inch seam allowance all around. Do you see how long the points are compared to the actual seam allowance you need?

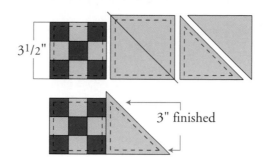

This triangle will fit correctly.

Add $\frac{7}{8}$-inch to the finished size of your square. If you cut in metric, but sew with a $\frac{1}{4}$-inch seam allowance, add just shy of 2.25 cm to the finished size.

Regardless of the size of the square, $\frac{7}{8}$-inch is the magic number!

But We Digress
Let's get back to the bed-size quilt under discussion. When $\frac{7}{8}$-inch is added to $5\frac{1}{4}$ inches, the size square you need to cut is $6\frac{1}{8}$-inch. Of course, you would first cut strips $6\frac{1}{8}$-inch wide, and then cut the strips into squares. This is where things are a little awkward, because most people work with a 6-inch wide ruler, not $6\frac{1}{8}$-inch.

Some people say just working with $\frac{7}{8}$-inch is awkward. It is true that it almost guarantees an odd number of eighths in your measurement, not the nice $\frac{1}{4}$-inch increments to which we are accustomed.

As quilting has become more popular, so has the availability of rulers, templates and paper-piecing methods that eliminate the points, or dog ears, and get around the odd eighths in some sizes. However, it is most helpful for you to understand the magic $\frac{7}{8}$-inch so you can understand when to use it and when to give it up.

Pairs of Pairs or Rows?
On page 24, we suggested using the pairs of pairs technique. However, for this quilt, it might be easier to keep the colors in position by completing horizontal rows.

If you choose rows, press the seam allowances directionally after the blocks are sewn into rows—press row one to the left, row two to the right, et cetera. The resulting ridges become grippers for sewing the rows together, and will probably eliminate the need for most pinning.

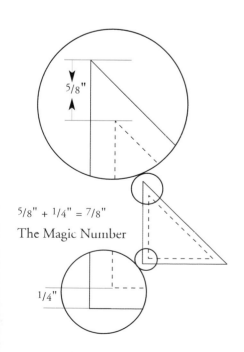

$\frac{5}{8}" + \frac{1}{4}" = \frac{7}{8}"$
The Magic Number

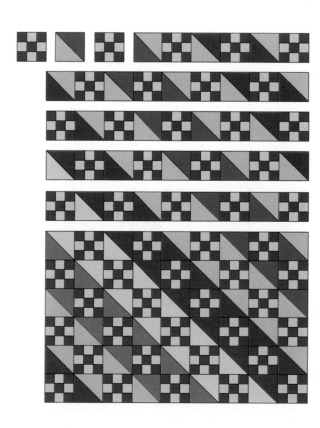

88 Nine Patch Arrows

Nine Patch Block

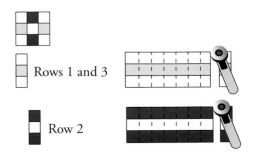

Rows 1 and 3

Row 2

This 5/2/1/1 arrangement of the Nine Patch makes the arrows possible. There are four arrows per block. Do you see them?

Cut triangles from squares.

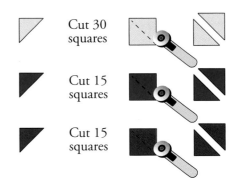

Cut 30 squares

Cut 15 squares

Cut 15 squares

 If this square is 1", the finished size is 25" x 29¹/₄".
If this square is 2.5 cm, the finished size is 62.5 cm x 73.1 cm.

 The arrows are so dominant that it would be easy to look at this quilt and automatically think the Nine Patch blocks are alternated with the "X" blocks in a diagonal set.

Well, you could make this quilt like that—but most people prefer sewing rows in a straight set, so this quilt is our introduction to the mock diagonal set.

This Nine Patch is clearly on point. Instead of looking at the diagonal rows, look at this square sub-unit.

The blocks can be easily made and assembled without setting triangles or odd numbers of pieces in each row. Quilts that have the strength of a diagonal set without the extra work are a real joy to sew.

 Mock Diagonal Set
This mock diagonal set concept can be used in many different quilts. The only question, "What size are the corner triangles?"

Let's look for clues. We know that in this sub-unit, we want the legs of the corner triangles to be on the straight grain. That means cutting a square in half diagonally, just like the corner triangles on diagonal set quilts. (See page 78.)

We just reviewed why you add 7/8" to the size of a finished square to get half-square triangles. That magic number, however, is only magic when you know the length of one leg of the triangle—but we don't know that.

All we would know is the size of the Nine Patch block sitting on point in a new square. How can that help?

We discussed how to calculate the diagonal measurement of a square on page 82.

• The finished size of any square times 1.41 is equal to the diagonal measurement of that square.

• So if this Nine Patch is 3 inches, then 3 x 1.41 = 4.23, or almost 4¼ inches. Since the diagonal of the Nine Patch goes from edge to edge of the new square, 4¼ inches is also the size of the new block we want to make.

• The length of the leg of each corner triangle is obviously half of the new block, or 2⅛ inches. Add 7/8-inch to 2⅛ inches for the correct size square to cut for the half-square triangles. That is 3 inches.

• The formula for the size of the square that will be cut into two corner triangles is:

$$\frac{\text{size of 1st square x 1.41}}{2} + \text{7/8"}$$
$$\text{(Nine Patch block)}$$

Adding the Triangles

Add one triangle to the block. The triangle will have dog ears extending beyond the square on both edges. Press toward the triangle regardless of color. Add the opposite triangle and press the seams away from the Nine Patch. Add the other two triangles in the same way.

Design Your Own

89 Seeing Stars

If this square is 1", the finished size is 27¹/₂" square.
If this square is 2.5 cm, the finished size is 68.8 cm square.

If you used the design grid on the previous page, did you remember to try omission? If so, you might already have seen the stars. The trick of omission leaves every other Nine patch in the grid as an empty square. The square would be cut the same size as the Nine Patch. That begins to create a new diagonal grid in the quilt.

The next trick is a row of half blocks around the edges of the quilt. Instead of complete empty square, only half-square and corner triangles are used. An easy way to make the half blocks is to sew four triangles together.

When these triangles are colored to make an eight-pointed star around a Nine Patch set on point in a square, you are Seeing Stars.

Whether you like the multi-color arrangement, Seeing Stars, or the repetitive version with just four fabrics, Running Stars, you'll agree this simple quilt is very effective.

89a Running Stars

89b Not Running Stars

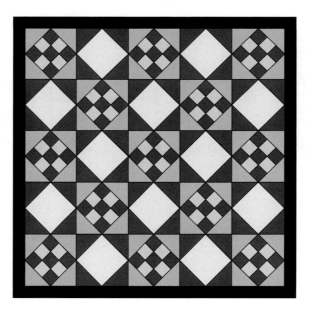

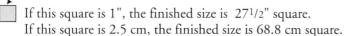
If this square is 1", the finished size is 27½" square.
If this square is 2.5 cm, the finished size is 68.8 cm square.

To highlight how important the last row of half blocks is to this design, we've duplicated Running Stars without the extra half-row. Notice how the stars almost disappear in Not Running Stars when the star points are not colored to extend beyond the row of Nine Patch blocks.

Design Your Own

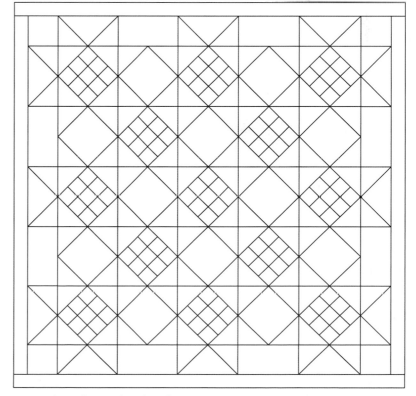

Reproduce this grid and make your own stars.

90 Windows on Point

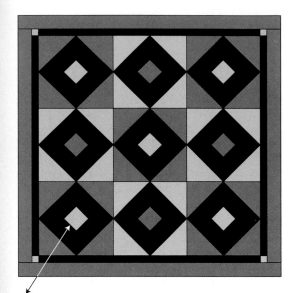

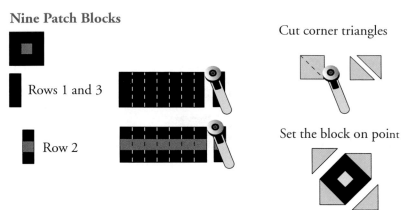

Nine Patch Blocks

Rows 1 and 3

Row 2

Cut corner triangles

Set the block on point

If this square is 1", the finished size is 14³/4" square.

If this square is 2.5 cm, the finished size is 36.9 cm square.

Remember Quilt 16, Nine Patch Windows? Here it is on point, except it is really a mock diagonal set. The grid for coloring both designs on this page is the same as the Nine Patch Arrows grid, page 115. The formula for the size of the squares to cut for the setting triangles, and the entire mock diagonal set technique, are the same—but the results are so different!

Starry Windows would be a wonderful scrap quilt to "build" on a design wall. Make a handful of the Nine Patch Windows blocks. Then cut light, medium and dark value corner triangles in sets of four or eight. All of the triangles are the same size beause they are all corner triangles.

Randomly arrange some of the sets of four around Window blocks and create star points with sets of eight. Allow the new star units to blend with each other, even sharing common corners. Fill in empty spots with more medium value "quilt" fabrics. When satisfied with the arrangement, assemble each individual Window block with

90a Starry Windows

If this square is 1", the finished size is 33⁵/8" x 37⁷/8".
If this square is 2.5 cm, the finished size is 84.1 cm x 94.7 cm.

four appropriate corner triangles. Then assemble these new units blocks using the pairs method on page 24.

91 Harlequin

If this square is 1", the finished size is 16¹/₄" x 21¹/₂".
If this square is 2.5 cm, the finished size is 40.6 cm x 53.8 cm.

Design Your Own

Add sashing strips and squares to the same Nine Patch on point unit for an entirely different look. The appearance of a diagonal set is gone.

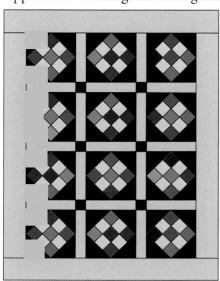

Instead, scrappy Nine Patch blocks sparkle in a sashing framework.

Change the value or arrangement of one component at a time and have fun making a series of these Harlequin quilts.

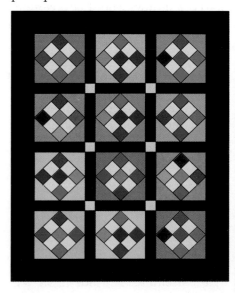

92 Snowball

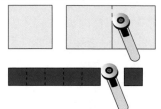

Cut Snowball units:

The Snowball Trick: Stitch corner to corner on small squares.

If this square is 1", the finished size is 33" x 39".
If this square is 2.5 cm, the finished size is 82.5 cm x 97.5 cm.

If this square is 1¹/2", the finished size is 49¹/2" x 58¹/2".
If this square is 3.8 cm, the finished size is 123.8 cm x 146.3 cm.

Cut Perfect Corners with Templates

To perform the Snowball Trick with templates, cut the big square the same size as the Nine Patch block. Choose a triangle template whose leg is the same dimension as the small squares in the Nine Patch blocks. Cut the shapes from pre-cut strips that are the correct width.

Position the triangles on the corners of the square, right sides together, so the match points touch the raw edge of the square. Stitch ¹/4 inch from the edge of the triangle, on the hypotenuse.

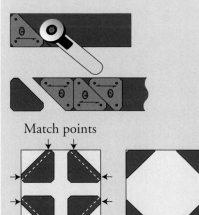

Match points

Nine Patches and Snowball makes a terrific overall pattern. Shown in two colors, this is also a really fabulous scrap quilt! To make the pattern work, the fabric in the four position of the Nine Patch blocks should match the actual fabric or the value of the fabric in the corners of the Snowball blocks.

Use the Snowball Trick of sewing small squares in the corners of a larger square and trimming the excess. Cut the large square the same size as

your finished Nine Patch plus ¹/4-inch seam allowances. Cut the small squares the same size as the strips you cut for the Nine Patch blocks.

If you own any From Marti Michell Perfect Patchwork Templates, you can use them to cut accurate corner triangles. There are lots of matching square-and-triangle pairs. (See Tip box).

93 Hidden Nine Patch

If this square is 1", the finished size is 30" square.
If this square is 2.5 cm, the finished size is 75 cm square.

Cut 13 blue squares and 12 red squares for star centers

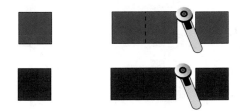

Make Flying Geese Sub-units
The sub-unit for the star points is commonly called Flying Geese. These units alternate with Nine Patch blocks to create the stars. Use your favorite method to make these sub-units, or construct them like the Snowball Trick on the opposite page. Sew squares to either side of a rectangle. Do this one square at a time, as the pieces overlap.

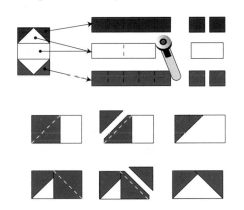

Put a soft gingham background behind the popular Variable Star by cleverly alternating easy-to-make sub-units. Many quilts in this book have included a Nine Patch block and a matching-size non-pieced square. At first glance, you might think this quilt does, too—but look more closely. The non-pieced square at the center of the stars is really two-thirds of the Nine Patch block. The easy way to calculate the size of this square is to add ¹/2-inch to the finished size of two squares in the Nine Patch block.

94 Checkerboard

If this square is 1", the finished size is 56" x 74".
If this square is 2.5 cm, the finished size is 140 cm x 185 cm.

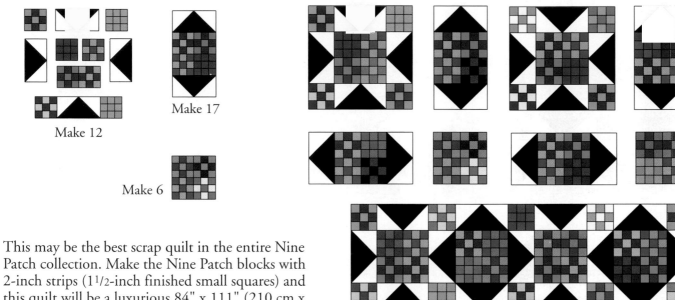

Make 12

Make 17

Make 6

This may be the best scrap quilt in the entire Nine Patch collection. Make the Nine Patch blocks with 2-inch strips (1½-inch finished small squares) and this quilt will be a luxurious 84" x 111" (210 cm x 277.5 cm) queen/double. That may sound a little long. If you want to, you can drop off a row or two, but you will lose the symmetry of matching corners because the design repeat is so large.

The connecting triangles are made like Quilt 89, Seeing Stars, page 116.

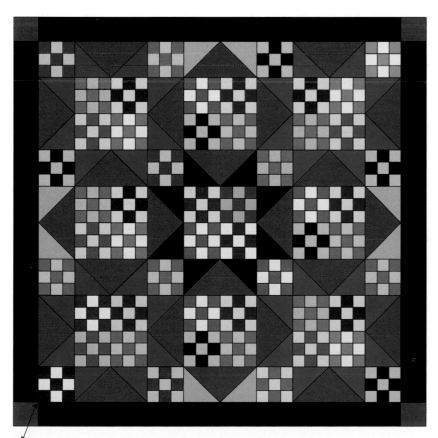

Wallhanging
Love the Checkerboard Star, but want something a little smaller? This would be a wonderful wallhanging.

If this square is 1", the finished size is 34" square.
If this square is 2.5 cm, the finished size is 85 cm square.

95 Goose in the Pond

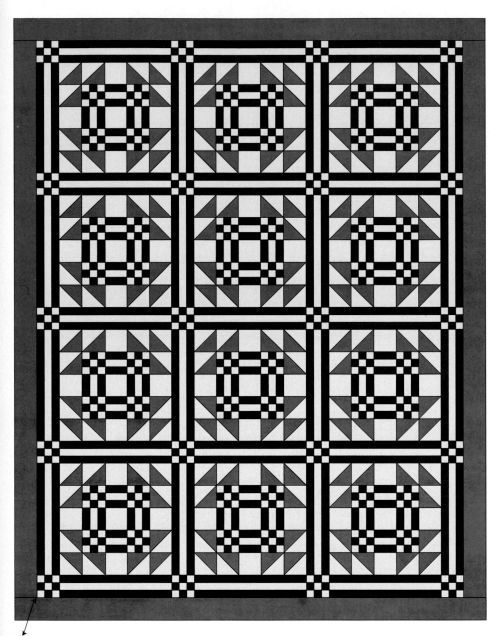

Fence Rail Blocks

Squares

Half-square Triangles

Cut squares the finished size of the Nine Patch plus 7/8".

Save time and improve accuracy by putting the two fabrics right sides together before cutting. (See "Make Sewing Easier" Tip page 112.)

Make 12 blocks.

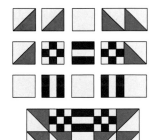

If this square is 1", the finished size is 63" x 81".
If this square is 2.5 cm, the finished size is 157.5 cm x 202.5 cm.

This Goose in the Pond is set together with sashing strips that match the Fence Rail blocks. Cutting these strips on the lengthwise grain will make the quilt go together more easily. (See Cutting Strips on the lengthwise Grain, page 19.) The sashing squares match the Nine patch units.

Make it in three colors as shown or have fun making every block a different combination. Let the sashing fabric and background fabric be consistent.

Design Your Own

Three-color Goose in the Pond

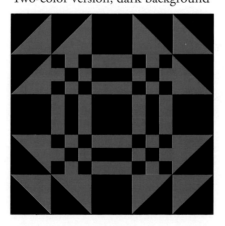

Two-color version, dark background

Two-color version, light background

95a & 95b Duck Blinds

The Duck Blind quilts appear to be two-color versions of Goose in the Pond, but no, not quite.

Color the center square and the squares in the center of each edge of the block to match the triangles and create Duck Blind.

Set the blocks together with sashing squares and sashing the width of two strips in the Fence Rail. This creates a wonderful secondary design, equally appealing with a light or dark background.

The poetic way of looking at these designs would be to think of the triangles as a flock of geese and the hidden squares as the hunters in the duck blinds—too covered up with greenery to get a clear shot of the ducks, anyway!

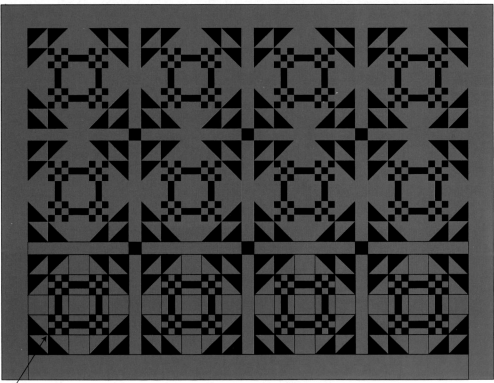

If this square is 1", the finished size is 57" x 74".
If this square is 2.5 cm, the finished size is 142.5 cm x 185 cm.

96 Nebraska

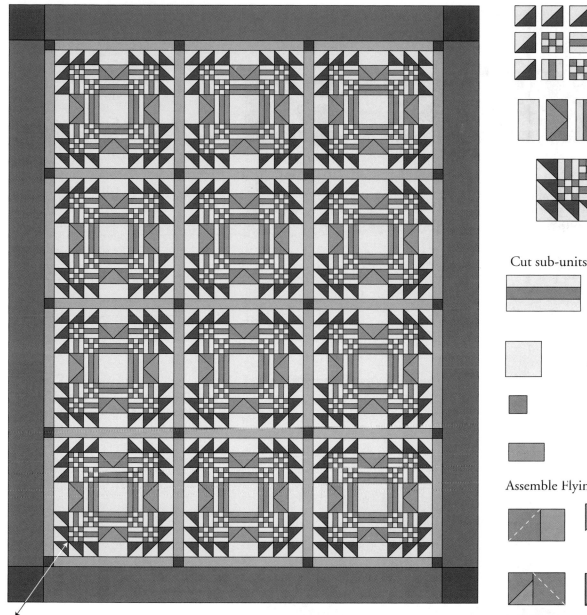

If this square is 1", the finished size is 80" x 106".
If this square is 2.5 cm, the finished size is 200 cm x 265 cm.

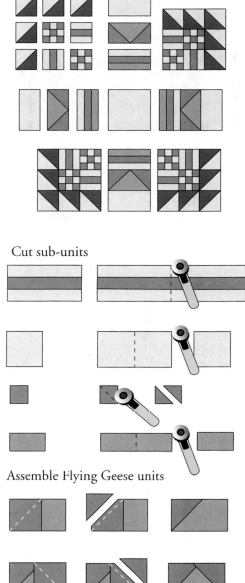

Cut sub-units

Assemble Flying Geese units

The Nebraska quilt is a grand finale of Nine Patch, Fence Rail, Flying Geese and half-square triangle sub-units. It is a classic pattern. Surely it is a case of one upmanship, developed by someone whose neighbor had made Goose in the Pond! If you aren't feeling competitive enough to make 3-inch Nine Patch blocks and the number of blocks shown for a bed quilt, consider these options:

• Make just one block; any size starting strip, from 1 1/4 to 2 inches, would make a nice wallhanging.

• Start with 2-inch strips and make only 6 blocks. Assemble 2 blocks by 3 and add borders. The quilt will still be approximately 80" x 116" (200 cm x 290 cm)

• Want it shorter? Eliminate the top border; it never shows.

The sashing strips are the width of two little strips in the Fence Rail.

97 Santa Fe Crossing

Goose in the Pond

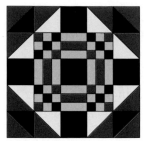

Santa Fe Crossing

■ If this square is 1", the finished size is 38" square.
If this square is 2.5 cm, the finished size is 95 cm x 95 cm.

Santa Fe Crossing is Goose in the Pond–it's hard to recognize. The block has been recolored dramatically and turned on point. When blocks are set on point, it usually means putting the same pieces together in a different way.

To make the partial blocks on each side, cut squares in half for the interior triangles so the grain will be on the legs. Cut setting triangles for the two triangles that are on the outside edge of the quilt (see page 78). It is easiest to use a whole Nine Patch block on the outside edges, also, and trim away the excess. Cut corner triangles from squares (see page 79).

Railroad Lanterns (*opposite*)
Isolate the on-point block from Santa Fe Crossing with setting triangles and alternate non-pieced blocks. Add a wide border (three times as wide as the Nine Patch) and you will have plenty of room for quilting.

98 Railroad Lanterns

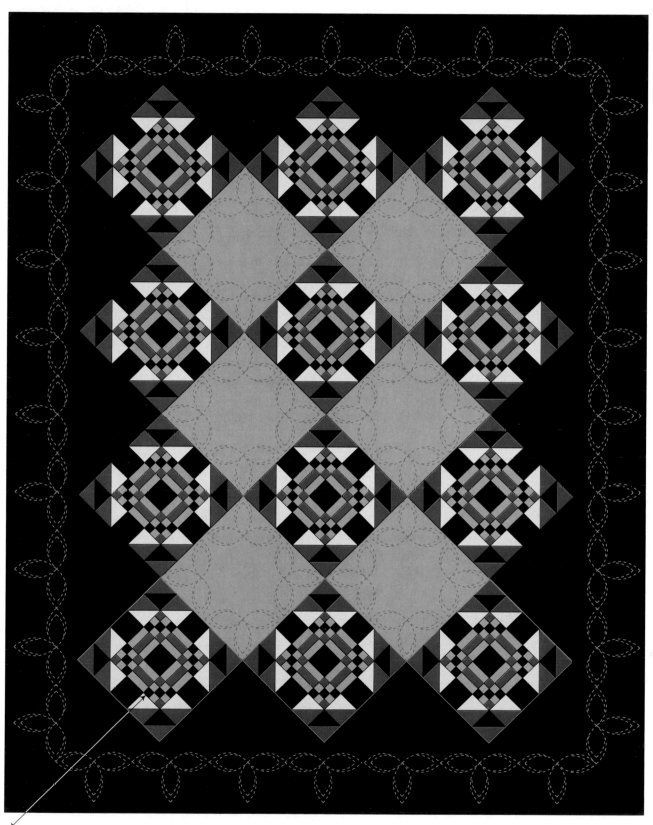

■ If this square is 1", the finished size is 72" x 93¹/8".
If this square is 2.5 cm, the finished size is 180 cm x 232.8 cm.

A Family of Chained Stars

The Nine patch block is a wonderful tool for linking other design units together. The next three quilts are great examples of that technique.

You will see these two star blocks in the quilts. They are slight variations of the Ohio Star and Elongated Star.

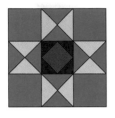 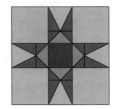

Each has empty corner squares just begging to be filled with Nine Patch blocks.

Chained Ohio Stars

To be effective, the dominant diagonal color must be positioned as in the diagram. That is, some of the Nine Patch blocks are 4/3/2, and some are the classic 5/4.

You can make Nine Patch blocks any size you want and you can cut the rest of the shapes in this quilt with the formulas noted earlier.

The quilt as shown is alternating Chained Ohio Star and Double Nine Patch blocks. Make the small square in the Nine Patch 1¹/2" (3.8 cm) finished and the quilt is 75" x 103" (187.5 cm x 257.5 cm), fine for a double bed, but you would need wider borders for a queen-size quilt.

Make 18   Make 17

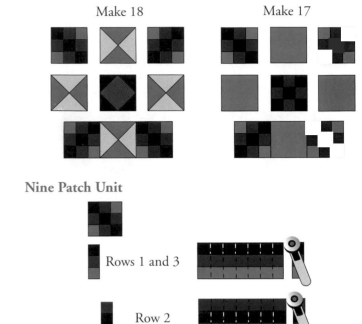

Nine Patch Unit

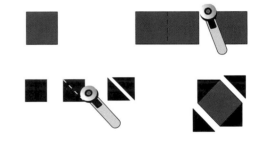

Rows 1 and 3

Row 2

Center Unit, Chained Ohio Star

See Quilt 88, Mock Diagonal Set, page 114.

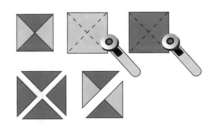

Side Unit, Chained Ohio Star

See The Secret of the Setting Triangles, page 78.

99a Chained Ohio Stars

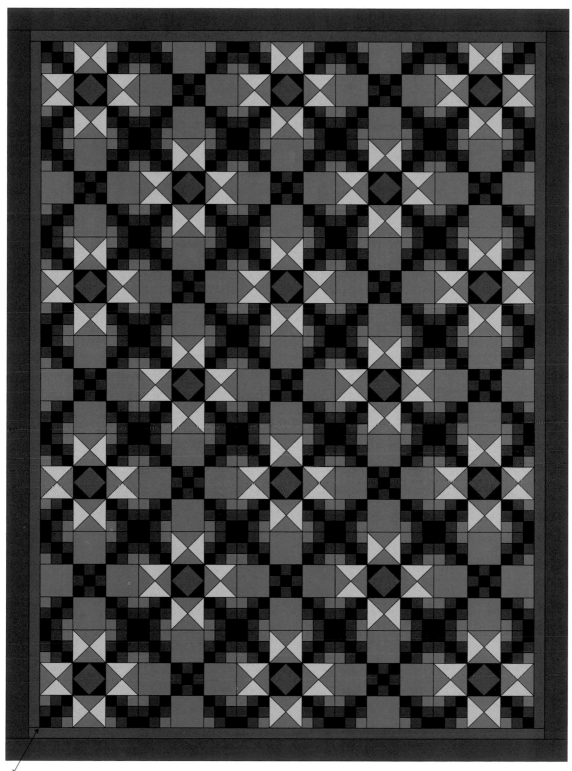

If this square is 1", the finished size is 51" x 69".
If this square is 2.5 cm, the finished size is 127.5 cm x 172.5 cm.

Starry Chained Nine Patches

The typical Elongated Star is made with nine equal-size squares. The four squares on the center of each side are divided into three triangles to make the star points. The shapes are easily drafted by finding the center of one side of the square and extending lines to the opposite corners. Add seam allowances on all sides.

Center

Rotary cutting these shapes is easiest with acrylic templates or a special ruler, but if those aren't available, just put your paper pattern down on the fabric and put the ruler on top to cut.

But wait–have you noticed this is not the typical Elongated Star? It still has nine equal squares, but they have all been pushed from the center out.

A small Flying Geese sub-unit has been added on each side of the center square. The corner squares have been enlarged and filled with Nine Patch blocks.

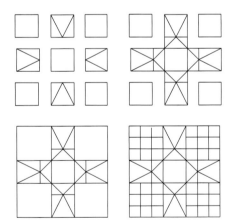

When you draft the star points, start with a square twice the finished size of the small Nine Patch square, not the same size as the Nine Patch. The Flying Geese sub-unit is the same strip width as the small square in the Nine Patch and twice as long. (See Hidden Nine Patch, page 121.)

The sashing strips are the same width as the Nine Patch strips.

Some quilts that feature such lovely interlocking designs become difficult to alter without losing the balance of the design. However, the Starry Chained Nine Patch is easy to alter. Take away or add a row of blocks at will. In the chart below, we have listed the approximate sizes when the number of rows and the size of the starting strips are altered. When you get close to the size quilt you want to make, it is easy to fine tune with borders.

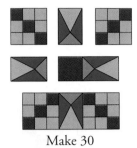

Make 30

Blocks across by down	Approximate Finished Sizes if the small square is			
	1 inch	1 1/2 inches	1 3/4 inches	2 inches
3 x 5	32" x 50"[1]	48" x 75"	56" x 87 1/2"	64" x 100"
3 x 6	32" x 59"	48" x 88 1/2"	56" x 103 1/4"	64" x 118"
4 x 5	41" x 50"	61 1/2" x 75"	71 3/4" x 87 1/2"	82" x 100"[3]
4 x 6	41" x 59"	61 1/2" x 88 1/2"	71 3/4" x 103 1/4"[2]	82" x 118"
5 x 5	50" square	75" square	87 1/2" square	100" square[4]
5 x 6	50" x 59"	75" x 88 1/2"	87 1/2" x 103 1/4"	100" x 118"
5 x 7	50" x 68"	75" x 102"[2]	87 1/2" x 119"	100" x 136"
6 x 6	59" square	88 1/2" square	103 1/4" square[4]	118" square
6 x 7	59" x 68"	88 1/2" x 102"	103 1/4" x 119"	too big
7 x 7	68" x 68"	102" x 102"[4]	119" x 119"	too big

All sizes include a border proportionate to that shown.
For sizes in centimeters, multiply by 2.54.

[1] Nice crib size, and the 1-inch square is a nice baby size.

[2] Both the 4 x 6 arrangement with 1 3/4-inch squares and the 5 x 7 arrangement with 1 1/2-inch squares would make nice twin-size quilts. The 5 x 7 has 11 more blocks and each block has 61 pieces, or 671 more pieces. Take your pick.

[3] 4 x 5 with 2-inch squares is a nice queen/double–you might want to add slightly larger borders.

[4] There are three quilts that could easily be made to fit a king-size bed. The 5 x 5 with 2-inch squares would be my choice, even though I would need to add extra border width. The larger piece is appropriate for the larger bed, and requires half as many pieces as the 7 x 7 arrangement.

99b Starry Chained Nine Patches

If this square is 1", the finished size is 50" x 59".
If this square is 2.5 cm, the finished size is 125 cm x 147.5 cm.

99c Chained Stars and Log Cabins

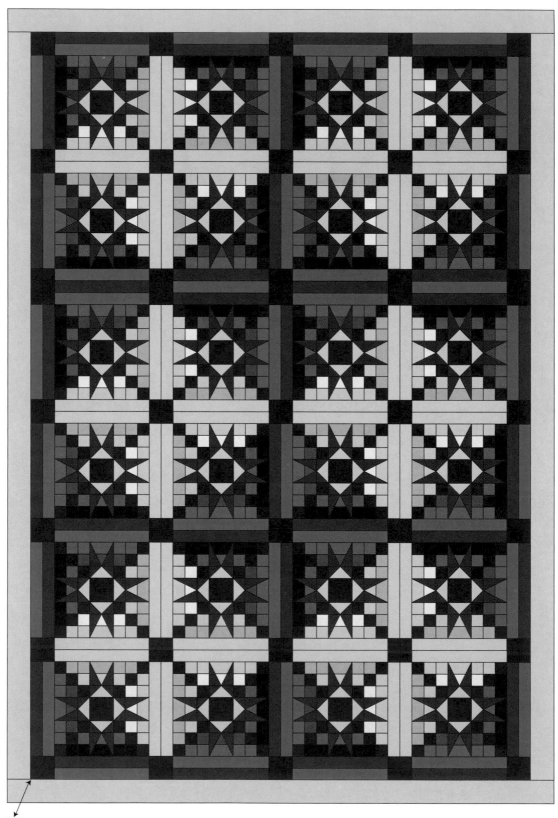

If this square is 1", the finished size is 46" x 66".
If this square is 2.5 cm, the finished size is 115 cm x 165 cm.

Chained Stars and Log Cabins

With just a little more detail, it really looks like Starry Chain is superimposed on a Log Cabin background.

How to Make the Block

This is just like Starry Chain except the coloring of the Nine Patch blocks is much more varied and the construction of the squares with the star points is different. In that unit, the broad triangle needs to be pieced or cut from two strips sewn together.

Then the blocks are framed to complete the Log Cabin illusion. Four blocks are rotated to create a new design unit.

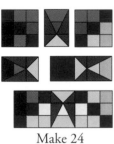

Make 24

How to Alter the Size

In Starry Chain, there is a long discussion about the ease of changing size one block at a time. In Chained Stars and Log Cabins, you have to remove or add four blocks at a time. This is the repeat unit:

For all practical purposes, this unit can be used alone, or two wide and three high, as shown, or 2 x 2 or 3 x 3. Any other variations are based on the strip size. The idea can be used in different arrangements, just like Log Cabin blocks can be arranged in a myriad of combinations, but when four blocks are united, there aren't many more choices.

The 2 x 3 arrangement illustrated actually has 24 blocks, but it is being called 2 x 3 because four blocks function as a single unit. Make it with 1³/4-inch strips for a long queen/double quilt. A 3 x 3 repeat unit with the same size strips is a great king-size quilt.

Use the design grid below to try other combinations.

Design Your Own

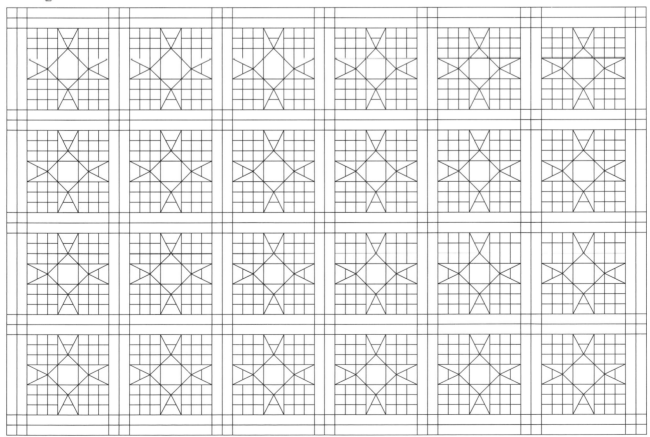

100 Honeybee

If this square is 1", the finished size is 30" square.
If this square is 2.5 cm, the finished size is 75 cm square.

The Honeybee is so sweet, it had to be included in a book of Nine Patch quilts. If you don't want to appliqué, then fuse the bees in place, and buttonhole stitch by hand or machine around the outside of the pieces.

Make the Nine Patch Block and Add Framing Strips
The framing strips are cut 2¹/2 inches (6.3 cm) wide for the small block and 3¹/2 inches (8.8 cm) for the large block. Add to two sides of the Nine Patch and cut to length.

Add final two sides and cut to length.

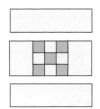

Appliqué or fuse the bees in place.

Add Sashing Strips
The sashing strips between the blocks are the same width as the first cut for your Nine Patch.

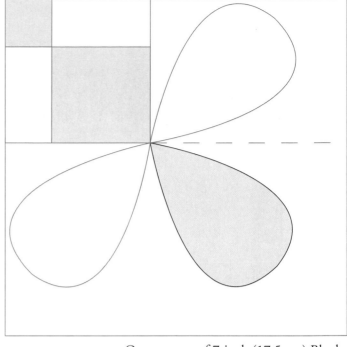

One-quarter of 7-inch (17.5 cm) Block

One-quarter of a 10½-inch (26.3 cm) Block

Full-size patterns for Honeybee block. Add seam allowance. Use your favorite appliqué method or fuse. Add seam allowance if needed. Use gray lines to mark placement for appliqué.

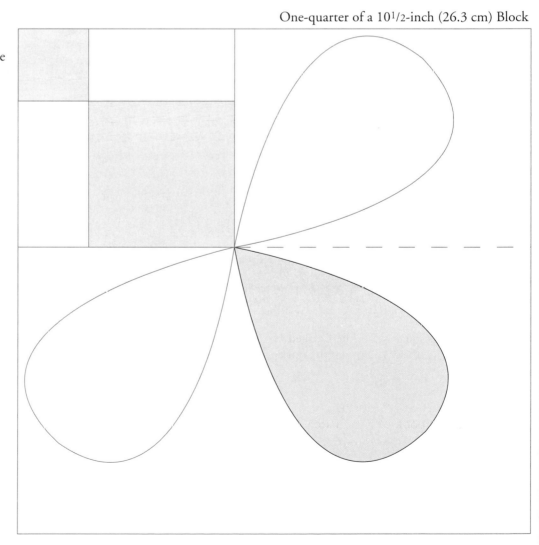

101 Jack's Chain

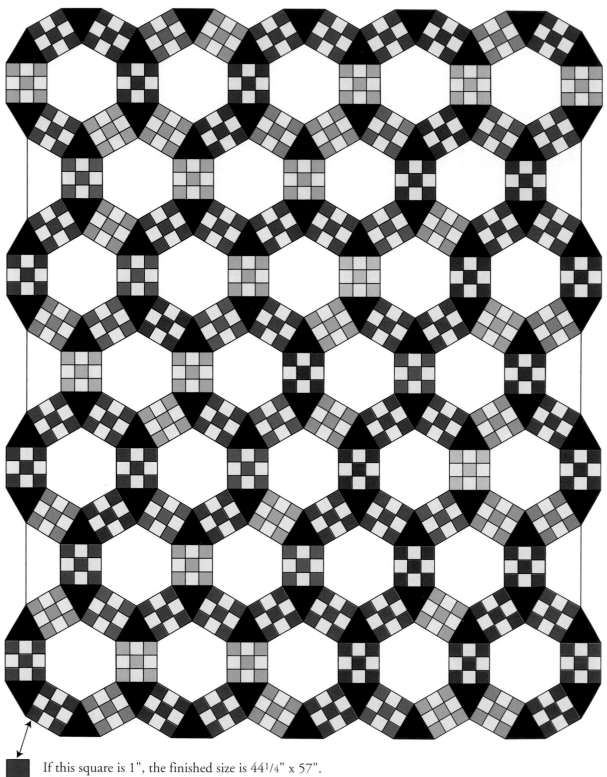

If this square is 1", the finished size is 44¹/4" x 57".
If this square is 2.5 cm, the finished size is 110.6 cm x 142.5 cm.

It is so unusual to have geometric shapes from both the 60-degree family and the 90-degree family in the same design, that it was a must to include, in fact a perfect No. 101!

Every Seam is Dot to Dot
Mark dots on hexagon pattern or template. (**Find pattern on next page.**) Dot-to-dot sewing is critical in the assembly of Jack's Chain, even on the Nine Patch!

Dot-to-dot means you never cross into the seam allowance. Leaving the seam allowances free is what allows you to reposition pieces and sew the unusual angles. Sewing beyond the dot is likely to cause puckering and poor fit.

Shorten stitch length as you approach the dot and it will allow you to more accurately stop at the dot as well as secure your stitching.

Stitch one triangle to each Nine Patch, dot to dot, and then add those units to the center hexagon.

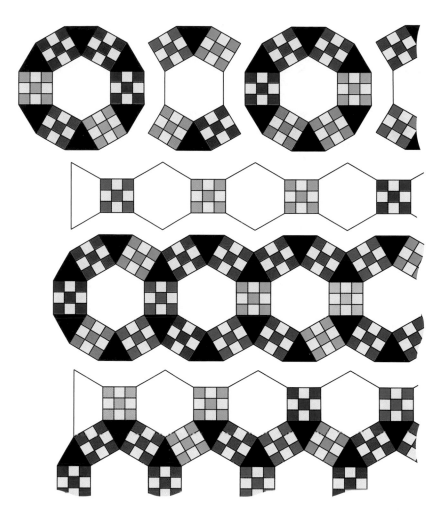

I like making circles and hour glasses instead of all partial blocks, for two reasons:

1. I can rotate a full circle during assembly to randomize colors better.

2. When the kids clean out the studio and find this unfinished project, they can make pillows or placemats from full circles!

(continued)

139

Jack's Chain Pattern

Full-size patterns for hexagon and triangle in two sizes. Add ¼-inch seam allowances and mark dots for dot-to-dot sewing.

Make Nine Patch blocks with 1½-inch or 2-inch cut strips.

One finished ring with 3-inch hexagon (we measure the length of a finished side) is approximately 11⅛ inches. With the 4½-inch hexagon, it is approximately 16¾ inches.)

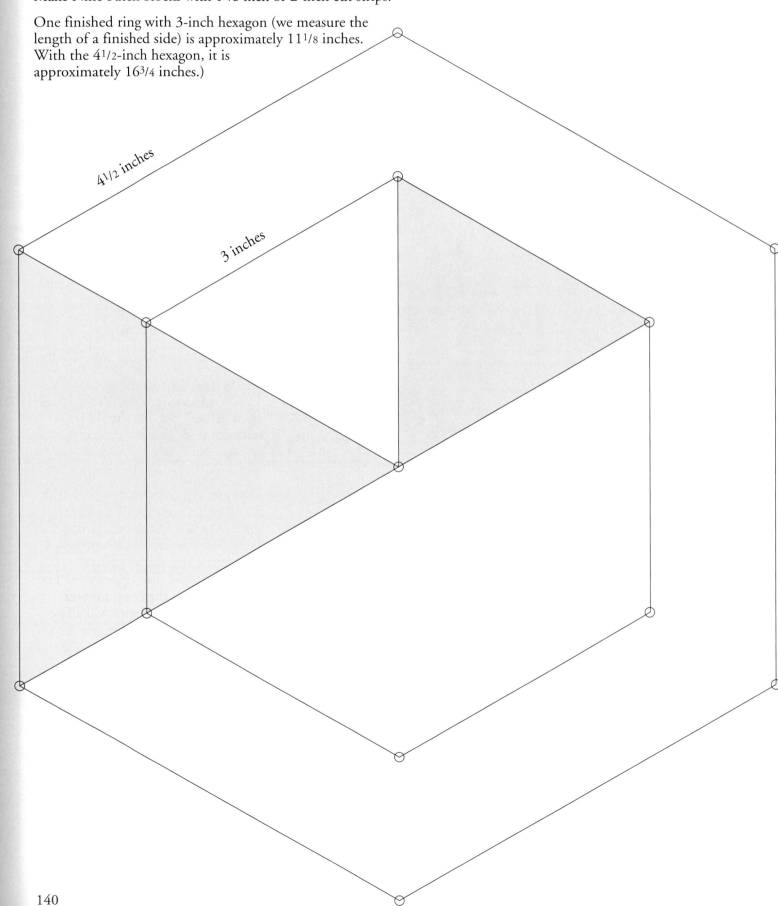

Finishing Your Quilt

When you have written as many quilt books as I have, this is the hardest chapter to write. While the quilts are always different, and there are new techniques represented in making the tops, there aren't many changes in how quilts are finished and writing the finishing chapter seems like warming over last nights dinner. But, it isn't a quilt until it is quilted so, to those of you who have been wonderful enough to buy several of my books over the years, I apologize if some of this seems familiar. Of course, just because you have bought some of my books doesn't mean you have actually read a finishing chapter before, does it? Just in case you have, there is a new tip in Machine Quilting in Sections, page 150; I have added the continuous binding method, page 154; and there is a label you can trace with a permanent ink pen, page 155. We probably should say, it isn't a quilt until it is quilted and has a label!

The Nine Patch Finish

The term "quilt" is loosely used to encompass all of the steps of planning and making a quilt. To quilt, the verb, is actually the process of holding together permanently the three layers that commonly make a quilt.

My opinion is that the quilting and finishing effort on a pieced or appliquéd quilt should be similar to the effort involved in making the quilt top. Therefore, since most Nine Patch quilts are rather easy to make, the finishing on them should also be easy. Of course, some Nine Patch quilts are designed with a wide open space intended for a beautiful hand quilting design.

Check the Size

In a Nutshell

Measure across the quilt interior in several places and along the sides to confirm equal measurements. Correct any irregularities before adding borders.

Finishing your quilt really begins before any borders are added. At that time, it is important to measure your quilt interior section carefully and accurately. Measure the length of the quilt from point to point, **Diagram A**. If the opposite sides match, great! Because you probably checked Nine Patch block sizes before assembling the quilt interior, the quilt sides will most likely match each other. However, if they don't match, make any adjustments needed now. If you don't correct an error now, it just gets more exaggerated with each border.

Diagram A

Traditionally, borders are added and a quilt top is completed before quilting. If you are adding borders this way, you may be able to adjust by easing the longer side of the quilt to the first border. Always ease the longer side to make it the same length as the shorter side; don't stretch the short side. If the quilt seems to ripple when you try to ease one side, it may be necessary to alter some of the quilt seams to correct the length. The goal is for opposite sides to be the same length.

Decide on the Border Type

In a Nutshell

In addition to deciding what styles of borders best suit your quilt, you have the opportunity to decide what technique of adding the borders best suits you.

If you thought all your choices were over when the blocks were made, think again! It is important that you feel free to design your own borders. The fabrics chosen and the set of each group of blocks strongly affect a quilt's look. The number and width of borders (and binding) that complement strong country colors may not flatter a pastel print version. Borders should be designed both to arrive at a certain finished quilt size, and to make the quilt as attractive as possible.

Type of border can refer to both technique (traditional, modified Quilt-As-You-Sew, etc.) and style (mitered, with corner blocks, etc.), **Diagram B**. The borders shown on the quilts in this book are all just suggestions. The fabrics you use, the size quilt you want and personal choice will all be more important in your border decisions than the illustrations or photographs of the quilts.

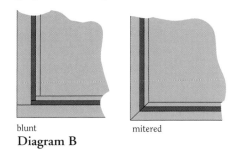

blunt   mitered
Diagram B

As the border types are described below, they include cutting and piecing instructions as part of the description, but before you cut any borders please read, Before Cutting Borders, on page 144.

Traditional Borders

Traditional borders are added to the quilt interior before it is layered with batting and backing; then the entire quilt top is treated as one unit.

Cutting Traditional Borders with Blunt Corners

Some people add extra length to their borders, "just in case." So I say, "Just in case, what? Just in case you decide you want a lop-sided quilt? No, no, no, cut your border strips the exact length they should be and make sure each border fits your quilt!" Mark and match the center point, quarter points and eighth points of both the quilt and the border strip, if necessary. If you cut any extra length and it gets unintentionally eased into the border, you are actually creating a ruffle. Granted, it has very little fullness, but as soon as the border is fuller on the outside edge than on the seam edge it will never lay really flat again.

1. Measure your quilt to determine the proper length to cut your strips, including seam allowances and extra fabric necessary if you are piecing the border strips, page 145.

2. Determine the desired finished width of the first border, and add $1/2$ inch for seam allowances.

3. Cut two side border strips the determined width and length.

4. To determine the length of the top and bottom border strips, measure the new width of the quilt top (including $1/2$ inch for seam allowances). Cut two.

Adding the Remaining Borders

Repeat steps one through three for subsequent borders. Always attach the side border strips first, then the top and bottom. Complete one set of borders before starting the next.

The ends of each subsequent side border strip should line up with the ends of the previous top and bottom border strips. Subsequent top and bottom border strips should extend from end to end of the previous side border strip.

Cutting the Borders for Mitered Corners

You don't see many mitered corners on my quilts and even when you do, they are usually mock mitered. Mitered corners take more time, more fabric, more skill and lots more luck than blunt corners. Even more to the point, when the same non-directional fabric is being used in the entire border, the resulting corners look the same whether they are blunt-seamed or mitered, **Diagram B** (page 141). In addition, I have a Theory.

> **The Mitered Corner Quota Theory**
>
> I believe that we are all born with an unknown quota for the number of perfect mitered corners we can make in a lifetime. I would hate to be 85 years old and have a great floral striped border fabric that just had to be mitered and discover that I had used up my quota mitering something as undemanding as muslin. So I save my mitering for corners where it really counts.
>
> There is a corollary to this theory that says, "Only three out of four mitered corners can be perfect on the same quilt on the first try!"

Adding a Mitered Border

Borders that will be mitered have to be cut longer than blunt finish borders. When cutting blunt borders, the side borders are the exact length of the quilt, but the length of the top and bottom border strips is the total of the width of the quilt plus the width of two finished borders plus $1/2$ inch. That same extra length must be added to all four border strips with mitered corners. Then they must be positioned perfectly and sewn to the side of the quilt stopping $1/4$ inch from the end of the quilt. Press the seam allowance toward the quilt top.

To stitch a traditional miter, the quilt is folded at a 45-degree angle

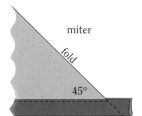

Diagram C

with the borders perfectly aligned on top of each other. Continue the fold line with stitching, **Diagram C**.

For a mock miter, work from the top of the quilt with one border extended flat and the other folded and pressed to make the perfect 45-degree angle. Pin in place and carefully stitch by hand with a hidden stitch, **Diagram D**.

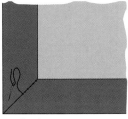

mock miter
Diagram D

When corners are completed to satisfaction, trim away the excess fabric and proceed. It is okay to miter one border, perhaps a demanding stripe, and not the others.

Cutting and Adding a Border with Corner Blocks

1. Cut two side border strips the desired border width plus two seam allowances, and the exact length of the quilt. Add as described in Adding the First Border, page 143.

2. Cut four contrasting squares the same size as the cut width of the border.

3. Cut the top and bottom border strips $1/2$ inch longer than the width of the quilt before borders. Add one square to each end of the top and bottom border strips. Matching seams carefully, continue adding borders as described on page 143, **Diagram E**.

Quilt-As-You-Sew Borders

Many books I have written feature quilts made with Quilt-As-You-Sew blocks that are then finished with Quilt-As-You-Sew borders. The

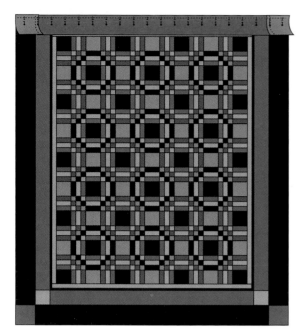

Diagram E

Diagram F

technique is like that described in this book under Machine Quilting in Sections, page 150. This is not frequently used unless the entire quilt was made using the Quilt-As-You-Sew technique.

However, after developing the Quilt-As-You-Sew border technique, the natural evolution was Modified Quilt-As-You-Sew borders.

Modified Quilt-As-You-Sew Borders

Instead of adding borders to the quilt and then layering and quilting traditionally, only the patchwork interior of the quilt is centered on the full size backing and batting. After that section is quilted, Modified Quilt-As-You-Sew borders are added to the quilt. They are added just as they would be traditionally, except that you will sew through the batting and backing at the same time. The point is you have to make a seam to add the border fabric to the quilt top, so why not quilt at the same time? In addition, it reduces the weight and bulk of the quilt while you are quilting the interior section.

Adding the First Border

1. Measure and cut borders as for traditional borders. Mark and match the center point, quarter points and eighth points of both the quilt and the border strip, if necessary.

2. Add both side borders first. Lay the quilt top on a large flat surface, right side up. Put one of the side border strips on top, right side down and one long edge aligned with one long edge of the quilt. Pin in place. Stitch 1/4 inch from the raw edge through all thicknesses, sewing and quilting at the same time, **Diagram F**.

3. Pull the border strips away from the quilt top. Pin or very lightly press the side border strips flat before sewing across the ends with the top and bottom border strips. Make sure the new corners are square and the opposite sides are equal lengths.

4. Add the top and bottom border strips in the same manner.

Adding the Remaining Borders

Repeat steps one through four for subsequent borders. Always attach the side border strips first, and complete one set of borders before starting the next.

Flaps Add a Special Touch

A flap is just that. In sewing terminology, it might be described as piping without the cord. A flap is used when you need a tiny bit of color as an accent or to delineate colors. Just as an extra mat with a tiny edge of color may be the perfect accent when framing a picture, a flap can be the perfect touch for a quilt. It can go between borders, or it can be used just before the binding.

While the flap looks like it is just tucked in between two layers of fabric when a seam is sewn, it isn't. It must be added separately, just like a border and in the same order as the borders, or the corners won't overlap correctly.

1. Cut a strip of fabric on the lengthwise grain, twice as wide as the desired finished width of the flap, plus 1/2 inch for seam allowances. The most common width of flap that I use is 1/4 inch, which means I cut a strip 1-inch wide.

2. Fold and press the strip in half lengthwise.

3. Line the raw edges of the flap up with the raw edges of the last section of the quilt, and stitch it in position,

Diagram G. Then proceed with the next border or binding.

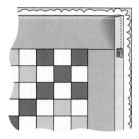

Diagram G

If you were stitching down both sides of a 1/4-inch border any deviation in the straightness of the seam would be very visible. That does not happen with flaps. The little bit of dimension that a flap gives is always very interesting. Although the flap does encroach 1/4 inch onto the section it is lying on, I have never found that to be objectionable.

Before Cutting Borders

In a Nutshell

Make borders most attractive for your quilt. Cut borders the exact length needed on the lengthwise grain when possible. If you must piece borders, use a diagonal seam.

Borders and Grainline

If there is one thing I'm adamant about, it is cutting strips on the lengthwise grain whenever possible. There is less fraying; there is less puckering in seams; and there is much added stability for pressing. Review Learning About Grainline, page 18. Please refer to the introductory chapter where reserving lengths of fabric for borders is discussed (**Diagram A**, page 18).

Economics may require piecing the border and binding strips, especially if the fabric is not used elsewhere in the quilt. When this is the case, I use minimal piecing, avoiding more than two seams in each strip. The following examples illustrate my train of thought.

Cutting Borders on the Lengthwise Grain without Breaking the Bank
Let's say I'm ready to put a narrow 2-inch border on a 64-inch by 80-inch quilt interior. Cutting the two 80-inch by 2 1/2-inch borders on the lengthwise grain with no piecing would require 2 1/4 yards of fabric, **Diagram H**, and there would be lots of leftover fabric. If I am willing to make one seam in each border (and why not, since you certainly have to piece a strip cut on the crosswise grain), only 1 1/4 yards of fabric would be required, but there would still be significant leftovers, **Diagram I**.

Cutting border strips crosswise and piecing them once would eliminate almost all the leftover fabric, and require only 5/8 yard of fabric, **Diagram J**. Even though borders cut crosswise are not as stable, there is one reason I'm willing to do this. Most narrow borders, like this 2-inch example, are not the outside or final borders. As long as the final border on a quilt is cut on the lengthwise grain, it will stabilize the quilt, and that is what counts the most.

In some books I give border yardage something like, "3/8 yard of fabric for the border, cut crosswise and pieced." That is not a command, only an explanation that to minimize the yardage needed, we calculated crosswise cuts. Please remember, if working from your fabric collection, cut border strips on the lengthwise grain whenever possible, and try to avoid more than two seams in a border.

The examples shown were for a very narrow border. As borders get wider, the fabric requirements increase and new ways of cutting borders on the lengthwise grain appear. The most common usable width of fabric is 42 inches/43 inches wide. One and one-quarter yards is 45 inches. If your fabric requirement is less than 1 1/4 yards and you plan to cut borders crosswise, consider these two options:

42"/43" wide

32" left-over fabric 2 1/4 yards long

Diagram H

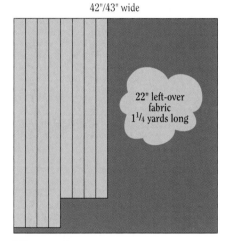

42"/43" wide

22" left-over fabric 1 1/4 yards long

Diagram I

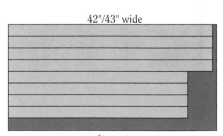

42"/43" wide

Diagram J   5/8 yard

1. Buy 1¹/₄ yards of fabric instead, and cut border strips lengthwise. There will be no more seams than when cut crosswise.

2. Buy the fabric requirement listed, but cut lengthwise anyway, just piece more.

If You Must Piece the Borders

If you must piece the borders or binding, place the pieces at right angles and stitch diagonally as if you were piecing bias strips, **Diagram K**. Diagonal seams are less visible in a border, and eliminate bulk in folded bindings.

For each diagonal seam in a pieced border, allow extra length equal to twice the finished width of the border, plus 1³/₄ inches.

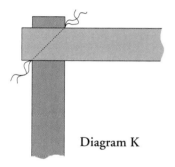

Diagram K

What About Backing Fabric?

In a Nutshell

> Consider piecing your quilt back for a pretty way to use leftover fabric.

Traditional quilt backs are usually made from one fabric with minimal piecing. Although most people piece two lengths for a full-size quilt with a lengthwise center seam, crosswise seams are okay, **Diagram L**. A single 42-inch/43-inch width of fabric will do for most crib and wall quilts.

Remember the possibility of pieced backs. They are fun and a great place to use any leftover fabric, especially if you are machine quilting and the bulk of extra seam allowances is as

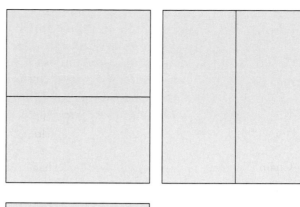

Diagram L

much concern as it is to a hand quilter. I'm not talking about piecing as elaborately as the front. It could be as simple as 18-inch wide vertical or horizontal strips of different fabrics, or 18-inch squares randomly pieced. You may have ended up with extra Nine Patch blocks or some that weren't perfect size. Stitch them into a strip or square and finish the backing with other odd fabrics. Just have fun and use up old fabric.

Selecting the Batting

In a Nutshell

> When making bed quilts with minimal machine quilting, my favorite batting is a medium-weight, bonded, soft polyester batting. For wallhangings, try the new lightweight polyester battings. Cotton battings are also very appropriate for wallhangings or for bed quilts with dense quilting.

What Kind?

My favorite batting for bed quilts with minimal machine quilting is medium-weight bonded polyester batting, sometimes called all-purpose. Batting that is very thin just won't puff enough—if it's too thick,

it is difficult to handle. Look for batting which is bonded through-out, because sur-face-bonded batting can sepa-rate when washed. Find a bonded batt that is reasonably soft. Suitable varieties are Hobbs Poly-down, Fairfield Light and many of the battings sold on a roll in fabric stores. Just make sure the roll batts aren't stiff. Machine quilting is stiffer than hand quilting, and a stiff batt results in a quilt that is just too stiff. The new cotton batts like Hobbs Heirloom are wonderful when I'm doing lots of quilting on a bed quilt, too.

Nine Patch quilts, especially scrappy versions might lend themselves to finishing with a tying technique, rather than quilting. Most people choose thicker bonded polyester batting for tied quilts.

For wallhangings, I often use the new lightweight polyester battings, such as Thermore® by Hobbs, or one of the new cotton batts, such as Heirloom® Cotton by Hobbs. These batts give the flatter look I prefer in a wallhanging, especially because I frequently add denser quilting, much of it free-motion, to the surface of a wallhanging.

Remember that batting choices are both personal and influenced by regional availability.

Preparing the Batting

As a rule of thumb when selecting packaged batting, choose the next size up from the size quilt you are making. The narrow width of most roll battings (usually 48 inches) is not a problem for most crib quilts or wallhangings. If you intend to use roll batting for a full-size quilt, you will need to shop for 80- to 84-inch wide roll batting or piece the batting. To do so, butt the lengths together then sew them with a diagonal basting stitch, **Diagram M**.

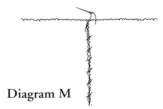

Diagram M

Remove packaged batting from its bag a day or two ahead of time so it can relax. A careful steam press eliminates humps and bumps. Put a lightweight fabric over either polyester or cotton batting to protect it from the hot iron.

Tying the Quilt

In a Nutshell

Tying the quilt layers together with yarn, or by using decorative machine stitching, is a quick and easy way to secure the layers of the quilt.

Tying may be used instead of, or in addition to, quilting. Several tying methods are suggested.

1. Hand tie the quilt with yarn. Use a large-eyed sharp-pointed needle with lengths of yarn as long as you can comfortably work with. Take a stitch in the center of each square or between the first pair of quilt blocks. Do not cut the yarn; leave a loop between stitches as you continue making stitches across the quilt. Then clip the yarn between the stitches, **Diagram N**. Pull the yarn taut to be sure it is not loose on the underside of the quilt. Tie in a square knot and trim the ends as long as desired. I like to leave the ends about 1/2 inch long.

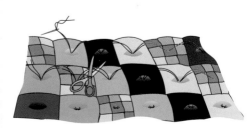

Diagram N

2. If you want to simulate a quilt hand-tied with ribbon, cut a 3-inch to 6-inch length of ribbon for each quilt block. Tie the ribbon into a bow, center it on the block and secure to the quilt with a narrow zigzag stitch across the bow.

3. Use a machine zigzag stitch, with both the stitch width and length set close to zero. Hold threads behind the needle, and stitch several times through all layers. This will secure the threads. Then adjust the stitch width to about 1/4 inch wide and stitch eight to ten times; then adjust back to zero, and stitch a few times more to secure the threads. Trim loose ends.

4. If you have decorative stitches available on your machine, experiment with a decorative stitch instead of zigzag. This is especially easy if you have the ability to instruct your machine to stitch one complete design and then stop. It is especially fun with some of the cute designs available.

Marking the Quilting Design

In a Nutshell

Marking and removing marks are both time-consuming tasks! Make sure that the fabric in the quilt will be enhanced by carefully marked and quilted designs. Test your choice of tools and technique on scraps.

Marking Basics

In many ways, marking is more important for machine quilting than for hand quilting. With hand quilting, you can stop and consider your options for the next stitch. With machine quilting, you are moving quickly and need to know where you are going. Frequent stopping and starting interrupts your rhythm. Remember that it is much easier to mark a quilt before it is layered. Therefore, the marking must be able to withstand handling and still be visible during the actual quilting.

To me, the first rule about quilting marked designs is to select fabrics that will be enhanced by rather than hide the quilting. To show off quilting to advantage, use solid-color fabrics, very minimally printed designs, and/or contrasting thread.

Marking Tools

If one marking method were perfect for every person and every quilt, there would only be one tool. This, however, is not the case. There are many different tools, each with advantages and disadvantages, and new ones frequently come on the market. My advice is to try whatever looks good to you. Each of us has different eyesight, lighting level at the sewing machine and preferences. In spite of the dozens of marking tools available, I have never become obsessed with trying them all. Generally, I use the water-erasable marking pens on light or medium colors, and a white chalk wheel or a silver pencil on dark fabrics.

Removing Marks

No matter which marking tool you choose, always test it on the fabric being used to make sure the mark is removable, and, no matter how you mark, mark as lightly as possible. Even chalk, which normally brushes off, should be tested to make sure it comes off easily.

Every quilter I know panics if a mark is not easily removed. Yet, as a collector of antique quilts, I see people almost reverently look at antique quilts with visible pencil marks and say, "Oh look, it has never been washed!" So, who knows? If the marking doesn't come out of your quilt, maybe a collector in the next century will consider it special.

Some people worry about the long-term effect of the water-erasable pens. I've heard the horror stories, but have always felt that the convenience and ease of use outweigh the risk. I have been using water-erasable pens for 20 years with no disaster. The best advice is to follow the instructions, don't leave the mark on any longer than necessary, and remove the mark thoroughly. Don't allow the marked quilt to come into contact with heat from an iron, a clothes dryer, or even sunlight streaming through a window; even gentle heat has been known to set marks. If you are really concerned, completely submerge the finished quilt in cold water, without soap or any other additive that might react with the marking. Soaking the quilt like this should remove the marks and prevent color that could reappear later from hiding in the batting.

Tip — *Correcting a Marked Line*

To correct a line marked with a water-erasable marking pen wet the line with a cotton swab to erase. When the fabric is dry, repeat drawing the line. Do not apply heat to speed the drying process, as this may heat-set any residue from the marked lines.

Practice Marking

If you are using a design that must be marked on the quilt, practice marking the design on newsprint first. That way you can confirm how long the repeat is, practice turning a corner, and figure out how to stretch or squeeze a design to fit a certain space before you start marking your fabric.

Using a Light Table

If you do a lot of marking and don't already own a light table it may be time to invest in one. The light illuminates the work surface from underneath, allowing you to trace a printed design directly onto fabric without using a stencil. It works as long as the fabric is not too dark.

You can create your own light table by laying a translucent acrylic panel over the opening of a leaf in an extension table. Place a light source under the table, and place your fabric on top of the acrylic panel.

Using Stencils

Plastic quilter's stencils are worth using when you want to mark a design on the surface of a quilt repeatedly and accurately. The narrow-cut section of the stencil guides the marker, while the solid area protects the quilt from stray marks. Extremely long cuts are broken up by bridges, or small connecting areas, that keep the stencil from falling apart. If you want a completely continuous line, it will be necessary to go back and fill in the areas you missed because of the bridges.

Precut stencils are readily available in quilt and fabric shops, at quilt shows and through mail order. The most common complaint about stencils is that if you've found an 8-inch design you really love, invariably, your block is 7 inches, which brings us to the next subject.

Making Stencils

To make your own stencil, draw the design actual size and mark bridges so that there are no free-floating solid areas. Trace the design onto the stencil template material (usually translucent plastic or Mylar film), and cut it with an art knife. Take care not to cut away the bridges. Cutting is made easier and more accurate if you use a double-bladed knife, which lets you cut both edges of the channel simultaneously. Another tool, similar to a woodburning device, is used with a special plastic material to make quilting stencils.

Introduction to Machine Quilting

In a Nutshell

I love both hand and machine quilting. I also love piecing. A stack of unquilted tops has very little appeal. The solution for me is more machine quilting.

I love hand quilting - both looking at it and doing it. Hand quilting afi-

cionados, and quilters who have hand quilted anything, have a great appreciation for the hours of work involved. The uninitiated, however, almost invariably looks at a hand-quilted quilt, then look at you and say; "Did you do that by hand?" You beam, "Yes," and then simply cannot believe the next question. "Couldn't they invent a machine to do that?"

They have. It's a sewing machine. You can't, of course, use any machine to make a hand stitch. The sewing machine stitch doesn't look like a hand stitch either. But until you get within a few feet, or sometimes inches, of a quilt, what you see is not the stitching, but the shadow created by the quilting indention. Machine quilting actually gives a crisper indention.

While I love hand quilting, I love making quilt tops more. I've learned that there is little personal satisfaction in a pile of unquilted quilt tops. I also love having people use my quilts. I can do that with much more emotional ease when the quilts are machine quilted.

In the early years of the current quilt revival, machine quilting would hardly have been considered, but many people are more realistic today. Thinking about appropriate applications for machine quilting will change your life. Remember that everything is a trade-off. Piecing and quilting by hand, because it was once done that way and that is what you want to reproduce, is fine. Making quilts entirely by hand in order to make it a "real quilt" is not legitimate. Machine quilting is real. In fact, machine quilting may take more skill than hand quilting, but it is a different skill. It is also much faster. The quilter who can be comfortable with machine quilting will be more productive.

The straight design lines of the quilts in this book are perfect for straight-line machine quilting. At the same time, there are many opportunities for free-motion quilting. It is a wonderful way to add interest and texture to borders. While hand quilting can enhance any of the Nine Patch quilts, the overall graphic designs can stand alone without really missing the hand quilting. Refer to page 152 for more information on hand quilting.

Layering the Quilt

In a Nutshell

This step is crucial, as the way the quilt is layered will become permanent. The object of this exercise is to center the quilt top on top of the batting that is centered on the quilt backing. In addition, the goal is to do so with no wrinkles or bubbles, and to secure the three layers together in a temporary fashion that can be removed when the quilting is complete.

If at all possible, do this step with a friend. It is so much easier with two people that you can layer one quilt for each of you in much less time than one person could layer two quilts.

Start with a freshly pressed quilt top, quilting design marked if necessary, backing, and a prepared (flat) batting. I would love to layer on a waist-high flat surface as big as my quilt, no stooping or kneeling! My substitute is a long folding lunchroom table. Whatever surface you use, it should be smooth and impervious to pin pricks. I want a high table, but lacking that, I now have a matching set of four cement blocks. The table is lifted up on the blocks for layering quilts or when there is lots of cutting to do. It can be lowered again for writing.

1. Measure and mark the center of both ends of the table with tape before you begin. Fold the backing in half lengthwise, then crosswise (into quarters), wrong side in. Mark the center of each edge at the fold lines. Do the same for the batting and quilt top, except fold the quilt top right side in.

2. Lay the folded backing fabric on the table, right side up, and unfold once. Align the lengthwise fold with the tape markings on the table, and pull the fabric smooth. Without shifting the fabric, open out the remaining fold. The backing should then be wrong side up, and hanging evenly on all sides of the table.

3. Lay the folded batting on top of the backing so it covers one-quarter of the surface. Use a ruler to be certain that the quarter-folded center corner matches the center of the backing. Unfold the batting.

4. Lay the folded quilt top on top of the batting, matching centers, and unfold it in the same way. The right side of the quilt top should be face up. Double-check all around the table to be sure that the three layers are even and centered. (Use telephone books or other weights to hold things in place.)

Pinning the Layers Together

In a Nutshell

Securing the layers together with #1 safety pins is my choice, no basting!

A minimum number of 350 safety pins are required to pin-baste a queen/double bed quilt; a crib quilt takes at least 75. I prefer the rust-proof chrome-plated #1 pins. Straight pins are not an alternative because they catch on the quilt and scratch you badly as you are working. Hand basting is more disruptive with one hand under the quilt and takes longer. Some of my friends have adopted the new quilt tack tools with enthusiasm. Ask at your favorite shop for a demonstration if you are trying to decide whether to invest in safety pins or the tool.

Think about your quilting plan so you avoid pinning where you intend to stitch. Start in the center and work your way out, pinning approximately every 4 inches. I recommend using more pins than you think you will need, and using less when you are more experienced. Pin from the top of the quilt, when the pin hits the table top, reverse direction; don't try to put your hand under the quilt to guide the pin. If you put your hand under it, the quilt is no longer flat.

When the first line of pins is secure, put one hand on the center of the table, and reach under the quilt to the backing and gently tug to make sure no wrinkles or folds have developed.

Each time you must re-position the quilt to pin a new section, check the back to make sure no wrinkles are developing. When you have finished pinning the entire quilt, turn it over and check the back to be sure it is as smooth as possible.

Folding the Quilt

The trickiest part of machine quilting is fitting an enormous bulky quilt under the comparatively tiny arch of a sewing machine. The only way to handle this is to make the quilt smaller and more manageable. The lengthwise center seam will be the first place to quilt. Before sewing, I roll the right side of the quilt to within 4 to 5 inches of the center seam. Fold the left side in 9-inch to 10-inch folds to within the same distance from the seam, **Diagram O**. Then, roll the quilt up like a sleeping bag, starting at the end opposite from where you want to start sewing, **Diagram P**. Now you are in control.

I hate to be the one to have to tell you, but you have to re-roll the quilt for nearly every seam. Sometimes, I can roll a quilt like a scroll without removing it from the machine. Machine quilting goes in fast, but it isn't fast to take out. You want to stay in control of the quilt. Getting sloppy with how you roll or don't roll your quilt is the easiest way to lose control. As you re-roll, check the quilt back for newly-sewn pleats. It's a personal decision, but I don't take out those little puckers most often found at seam crossings. If there's a tuck you could catch your

Diagram O

Diagram P

toe in, you have to correct it. In between is a gray area.

Setting Up the Machine

Nearly everyone wonders if they need a fancy machine to do the quilting. I have successfully machine quilted with all kinds of machines from very simple to the most expensive. Check your machine's quilting I.Q. on scraps first. If you have any problem, or don't like the look of the stitch, the first thing to check is the pressure of the presser foot. Too much pressure can make an undesirable rippling effect. Nearly every machine has an even feed attachment available that helps move all layers through the machine at the

same rate. One brand of machine even has a built-in even feed, which, I must admit, is my favorite for machine quilting in-the-ditch.

For most of the in-the-ditch quilting, I like to use invisible nylon thread for the top thread only. In the bobbin use a cotton or cotton-wrapped polyester thread that matches the color of the backing fabric. Today's monofilament nylon thread is not at all like the 1960's version of thick nylon thread that resembled fishing line. The new thread is more like slightly coarse hair (ask for size 80 or size .004), and comes in two colors, smoky and clear. I use smoky for everything but the lightest fabrics. The clear seems to reflect light and show more than the smoky. If I will be stitching on or beside only one color of fabric, I prefer to use the 100% cotton thread on the top also.

It is usually necessary to loosen the tension for the nylon thread. It is very stretchy and if the tension is too tight, the thread stretches while sewn and draws up and puckers when you stop sewing. I like a stitch length of eight to 10 stitches per inch for quilting.

One of the things that has made machine quilting so much fun in the last few years is the explosion of wonderful threads. Shiny rayon, metallics and textured threads can all add to the surface design of the quilt.

Machine Quilting

In-the-ditch Quilting

"In the ditch" refers to stitching in the space created between two pieces of fabric that are sewn together. Granted there isn't much space, so you create a little more space by pulling the fabric on each side slightly away from the seam just before it passes under the moving needle. That slight tension creates an extra-narrow channel for stitching. When your fingers release the tension, the fabric returns to its natural position

and tends to hide the stitching "in the ditch."

1. Roll the quilt and place the exposed end of the lengthwise center seam under the sewing machine foot. Pull the quilt away from the seam with both hands to make a ditch. Position a friend or table behind the sewing machine to catch the quilt as you sew; if it is not supported, the weight of the sewn quilt will pull too much on the unsewn part of the quilt.

2. Reroll the quilt and stitch the center horizontal seam. Stitch the remaining seams. I usually do two horizontal seams, one on each side of the center seam, then switch back to the vertical seams. Work out from the center, re-rolling the quilt before each seam.

If you added your borders traditionally, quilt in the ditch between each border.

3. Clip the threads and remove the pins. If you are using traditional borders, the quilt top is finished and ready for binding. Otherwise, now is the time to add the modified Quilt-As-You-Sew borders.

Straight Stitching on the Surface

Incorporate regular or straight machine quilting on the surface of the fabric, rather than in the ditch. The only difference is that you have to make a design or have a plan for the quilting, and the stitching is not hidden in a seam line. Follow a printed design in the fabric or mark a pattern, but minimize curves and eliminate as many turns as possible. Save them for free-motion quilting.

Free-motion Quilting

Straight-line quilting on the machine is really quite simple once you understand how to control the quilt and make it manageable. But what if you want to quilt in circles? Traditional sewing, where the feed dogs pull the fabric through the machine, would require somehow rotating that whole quilt around and through the machine. No way!

So what happens if you disengage or lower the feed dogs? Well, basically, the needle goes up and down, but the machine doesn't move the fabric. That means you become the power moving the quilt under the needle, and you can move it any direction you want, even in circles. The good part is you don't have to pivot the quilt around the needle!

That is why free-motion quilting is done with the feed dogs down. Most people like to replace the regular presser foot with the round embroidery or darning foot. When the presser foot is lowered, the darning foot doesn't actually touch the fabric, but it identifies where the needle will be stitching and is a safety buffer for your fingers. Even if you decide to stitch without a presser foot of any kind, the lever for the presser foot must be lowered as that is the same action that controls the tension on the upper thread.

Free motion means what it says. You can stitch any direction you want. An effective, but very easy way to do free motion quilting is random movements that create a stippled effect. However, if you want to try fancy feather quilting on the machine, free motion is also the method you would use.

Keeping the fabric moving at a fairly calm steady pace and the needle moving fast seems to be the easiest way to keep your stitch length regular. The hardest thing to believe is that the faster you sew, the easier it is to do. Practice on a small piece of layered fabric, but remember, your stitch length will not have the same consistency as it does when the feed dogs and needle are completely synchronized.

The place you are most likely to get puckers in machine quilting is where two lines of stitching cross. A random motion that goes forward and curves back and cuts back again without actually crossing a previous stitching line will give you a nice quilted effect without puckers. Just a little practice and you'll be amazed at what you can do.

Machine Quilting in Sections

In a Nutshell

Consider machine quilting in crib-quilt size modules. It may make machine quilting more plausible. Use finishing strips to cover seams when joining sections. Add borders using the Modified Quilt-As-You-Sew technique.

The technique is applicable to nearly any full-size quilt. Many people are very enthusiastic about it because there are smaller sections to handle when doing machine quilting. If a quilt is just too big to comfortably machine quilt, assembling it in sections is the solution. Sections of the quilt interior are layered with backing and batting, then quilted, then joined together.

Before completely sewing the patchwork interior together and adding the borders to the quilt, divide the quilt interior into quadrants. They don't have to be equal in size, just have straight seams for combining later. At this point, your quilt will seem like four little crib quilts. Cut four backing pieces and four separate battings. Allow extra batting and backing on two sides of each quilt section for the borders if additional borders are planned.

Layer as shown. Roll the exposed batting and backing sections and pin before quilting, as shown in one section of **Diagram Q**. This will make the sections smaller, and will cover the batting to prevent it being caught while quilting. Machine quilt as desired. Unpin after quilting the interior and prepare to join the sections. Put the quadrants together with finishing strips. Add appropriate borders using the Modified

Quilt-As-You-Sew Technique, page 143.

Joining the Quilted Sections Using Finishing Strips

The layered and quilted sections can't just be joined with a simple seam without raw edges showing on the back. The seam allowance must be covered. If the quilting goes all the way to the edge of the sections, finishing strips are used to cover the seam allowance.

1. Cut finishing strips $1\frac{1}{2}$ inches wide and approximately 2 inches longer than the length of the sections to be joined. Press the strips in half lengthwise with wrong sides together. Cut the strips to match the backing fabric unless you want contrasting fabric for design reasons.

2. Lay two adjacent sections right sides together, lining up the block seams carefully. Place a folded strip, with raw edges even with the quilt edge, along the seam line. Pin sections and strip together. Machine stitch $\frac{1}{4}$ inch from the edge through all eight layers. Refer to **Diagram R**.

3. Trim excess batting from the seam allowance, and press the strip to the side so that it covers the raw edges.

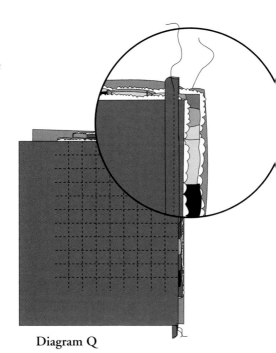

Diagram Q

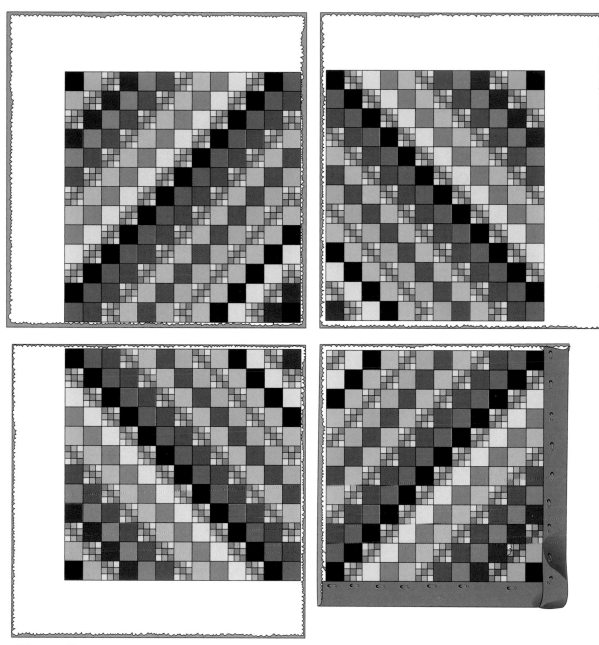

Diagram R

Tip *Batting Tip*

Eliminate batting from seams by stitching it to the backing 3/8 inch from the edge and trimming before joining the sections. This possibility is probably more useful with cotton batting than polyester. The cotton batting is denser and makes bulkier seams when stitched into the seams.

Hand stitch the strip in place, **Diagram S**. If you are clever with your sewing machine and don't mind the stitch showing on the finishing strip, this step can be done with your machine hemming stitch. Trim away any excess length of finishing strips before joining more sections or adding the binding.

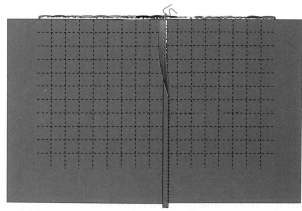

Diagram S

Hand Quilting

Hand quilting is a very portable way to quilt. Some people find handwork very soothing; some consider it the only "authentic" way to quilt. If you are trying to reproduce an antique hand-quilted quilt, it is; but that is not the only way to make a "real" quilt.

It is true that while pioneer women quickly converted to piecing by machine, they were more reluctant to quilt by machine. I believe that they pieced by machine, a project traditionally done alone, in order to have more quilt tops in less time. Then they quilted by hand, in groups, in order to preserve their social time. Quilting around the frame gave everyone a chance to hear the news, to gossip, and to express themselves with other adult women. Lucky the quilter, today, who has a group to quilt with around a large frame, because it is still fun and therapeutic.

Sometimes the combined use of machine and hand quilting is a logical response to different needs. Machine quilt in the ditch around large unit blocks and between borders, and then hand quilt inside the unit blocks. That approach lets the machine do the long, tedious but necessary stitching, while the handwork is done where it will show to best advantage.

The Technique of Hand Quilting

Experiment with different methods until you find one you like. Don't forget to get a comfortable thimble. The quilting stitch is a small, consistent running stitch. There is a lot of discussion about the appropriate number of stitches per inch. The beginner should look for consistency first, and strive for smaller stitches later. Hand Quilting can be done with or without a hoop or frame:

• **Full-size frame:** There are so many different frames, and each seems to be used slightly differently, so just follow the directions for the one you own.

• **Hoops:** Hand-held and floor-stand hoops are also readily available.

• **Without a hoop or frame:** Some people prefer quilting without the tautness of the hoop or frame, especially if they are quilting by the block and then assembling the quilt.

The Needle and Thread
Most people prefer to use a fairly small Betweens needle. In fact, they are so commonly used for quilting that Betweens are now often packaged as Quilting needles. I would suggest buying a package with assorted sizes and gradually work down to the smallest size.

In the past, most thread called "quilting thread" was intended for hand quilting only. Now there are some very nice threads labeled for either hand or machine quilting. The new quilting thread comes in a wide range of colors, but it is not as heavy as the traditional hand-quilting thread.

Bindings

In a Nutshell

My favorite binding is a separate French-fold binding, cut on the straight grain. The most common, but not only, finished width is 1/2 inch.

Stabilizing the Quilt Edge

Unless there is quilting very close to the edge of the quilt, it is a good idea to stabilize the quilt before adding the binding. Machine baste a scant 1/4 inch from the raw edge of the quilt top. Stitch through the top, the batting and the backing and stitch on all four sides of the quilt. Excess batting and backing will be trimmed away later.

French-fold Blunt Corner Bindings

For years, the French-fold binding with blunt corners is the only technique I have included in books. Because I make so many full-size quilts, and I never liked the idea of having to make 375 to 400 inches of continuous binding to go all the way around a quilt, I made blunt corners instead. In recent years, however, I have started doing the continuous binding on smaller quilts and will include those instructions after the blunt corner instructions.

A French-fold binding is double-folded and generally cut on the straight grain. It is cut four times as wide as the desired finished width plus 1/2 inch for two seam allowances and 1/8 to 1/4 inch more to go around the thickness of the quilt. The fatter the batt, the more you need to allow here. It is only necessary to cut this on the bias if the edge of the quilt is curved.

What Width and Length?
My favorite finished width is whatever size I think looks best on that quilt. Some quilts need a subtle narrow binding and others look best with a large, high contrast binding. The most common, however, is about 1/2 inch finished. With that width and an average full-size quilt, the equivalent of 5/8 yard of fabric is required for bindings alone.

To determine the length to cut the side binding strip, measure the quilt side. If you don't want to piece the binding, the strips need to be cut from fabric as long as the quilt. If you must piece the binding, do it diagonally as for piecing borders.

Adding the Binding

1. Fold the binding strip in half lengthwise with the wrong sides together and the raw edges even. Press. Binding strips are added in the same order as borders - sides first, then top and bottom.

2. Lay the binding on the quilt so that both raw edges of binding match the raw edge of the quilt top, and machine stitch in place.

3. Now is the time to trim away excess backing and batting, but how much? To determine that, pull one section of binding flat, so it extends onto the excess batting. Because I like full feeling bindings, I trim the backing and batting to be almost as wide as the extended binding. In other words, the extended binding will be about 3/16 inch wider than the backing and batting when trimmed, **Diagram T**. Assuming you started with a 2⁵/8-inch wide binding strip, and measuring from the seam, not the edge of the binding, the batting and backing would be trimmed 7/8 inch from the seam line or 5/8 inch from the edge of the quilt.

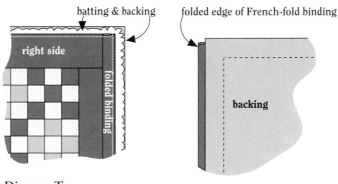

Diagram T

4. Roll the binding around the raw edge of the quilt to the back, and hand stitch in place using the row of machine stitching as a stabilizer and a guide, **Diagram U**.

Interestingly, even though I machine piece and machine quilt nearly every quilt, I still love a hand-finished binding. That is, it is sewn onto the right side of the quilt by machine, wraps around the edge of the quilt and is stitched to the back of the quilt by hand. The hand hemming stitch I use is hidden. The needle comes out of the quilt, takes a bite of the binding and re-enters the quilt exactly behind the stitch. The thread is carried in the layers of quilt, not on the outside.

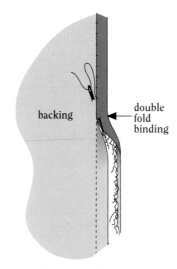

Diagram U

5. To make blunt corners complete the hand stitching on the sides of the quilt before beginning the end bindings. Trim batting out of the last 1/2 inch of binding before completing the hand stitching. Trim away in a staggered fashion other excess pieces of fabric so that the corners are not bulky and thicker than the rest of the binding.

6. Measure the quilt ends carefully. Cut binding strips, adding 1/2 inch at each end. To eliminate raw edges, fold under the extra 1/2 inch at each end, before folding the strips in half lengthwise. Continue in the same manner as above.

7. Complete the hand stitching for the ends of the quilt. At the corners, trim away enough batting and seam allowances to make the corners feel and look like the same thickness as

the rest of the binding. Carefully stitch ends shut.

A Machine-hemmed Binding
If you are hemming the binding by machine, attach the binding to the back of the quilt and bring to the front. When you are stitching the binding to the front, use the finished edge of the quilt as the positioning guide for the binding. When you are stitching from the back, the only guide is the stabilizing stitch that you made that is a scant 1/4 inch from the quilt top edge. Either draw a line 1/4 inch outside that stitching or lay the binding so that it extends over the stitching.

Bring the binding to the front and either top stitch with invisible thread or experiment with your machine hemming stitch. The hemming

stitch will take several straight stitches and then take a v-shaped stitch into the binding, **Diagram V**.

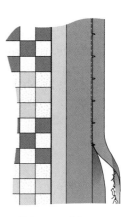

Diagram V

Continuous Mitered Corners

If you want to make mitered corners on the binding, everything is the same except you need to make binding to equal the total distance around the quilt plus about 12 to 15 inches.

1. Start in the middle of one edge with a diagonal fold and the raw end hanging off the quilt. Stitch binding to quilt as above. At the corner, stop stitching 1/4 inch from the edge of the quilt, **Diagram W**. Backstitch and remove the quilt from the machine.

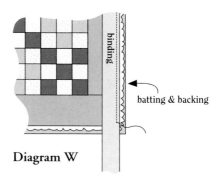

Diagram W

2. Fold binding away from the quilt, making a perfect 45° angle, **Diagram X**. Fold binding back onto next edge of quilt. The new fold should be even with the binding edge just sewn.

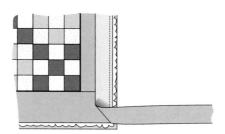

Diagram X

3. Start sewing again from the folded edge of the binding, **Diagram Y**.

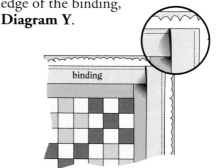

Diagram Y

4. Repeat at each corner. Overlap at starting point and trim away excess.

5. Roll binding to back and hand stitch in place.

Adding a Sleeve

The most frequently used method of displaying a quilt is to stitch a sleeve, or casing, onto the backing of the quilt so that a rod or dowel can be slipped through it. The rod and sleeve allow the quilt's weight to be distributed evenly, so that undue stress is not put on any part of the quilt.

1. For the sleeve, cut a strip of fabric approximately 7 1/2 inches wide, 2 inches longer than the length of the quilt edge.

2. Turn under a 1 1/2-inch hem at both short ends of the strip. Top stitch.

3. Fold the fabric in half lengthwise, with wrong sides together. Sew the long edges together using a 1/4-inch seam allowance. Press the seam allowance open, and to the middle of the sleeve, **Diagram Z**.

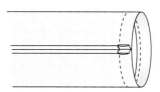

Diagram Z

4. Center the sleeve along one edge of the quilt backing, approximately 1 inch below the binding, with the seam facing the backing. Sew the sleeve to the quilt through the backing and batting, along both long edges, **Diagram ZZ**.

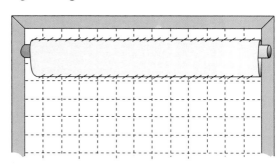

Diagram ZZ

It's Not Done Until It's Signed

I always urge quilt makers to sign their quilts, so that future quilt historians will know who made them and when. It is even more important to sign quilts that are made to be used, not preserved. Forget about the historians, sign and date the quilts you make for the people you know and love who will be using them. Signing can be as simple or as elaborate as you like, and can go on the front or the back.

As more sewing machines are featuring built-in alphabets along with other decorative stitches, making a quilt label is a great way to make use of the feature.

A really simple way to sign a quilt is to use an indelible marking pen or laundry pen to write your name, date and any inscription on a piece of pre-washed muslin or other fabric, and hand stitch it to the back of the quilt.

If you have made a quilt from this book, it would be wonderful if you would honor us by sharing that information with this label. Use a Pigma or other fine point permanent fabric ink pen to trace our label onto muslin. Decorate or embellish with colored inks or embroidery.

ABCDEFGHIJKLMNOPQRSTUVW
XYZ& abcdefghijklmnopqrstuvwxyz
1234567890

Swept Away by
101 Nine Patches

made by

for _____

date _____

Nine Patch Potpourri

Many "first quilts" are limited to two or three fabrics that "go with" the paint and carpet in the bedroom. Nine Patch quilts are a great "first quilt" choice. I think you will have seen many wonderful ideas in this book for two or three fabric Nine Patch quilts. If you paid any attention at all, you will have also noticed scrap Nine Patch blocks were frequently recommended. As beautiful as two and three fabric quilts may be, scrap quilts are still my sentimental favorite.

Scrap Nine Patch Quilts

Many people who love the look of scrap quilts are still intimidated about putting scraps together. They insist it is an acquired skill. They are probably justified in that claim. Anyone born before 1970 can probably recall his or her mother saying, "You can't wear that flowered blouse with that plaid skirt!" It must have been in the 1970s that we even began to put two coordinating prints together. The key word is "coordinating," because free-spirited combinations still weren't highly regarded. So, putting lots of prints together is a retraining process for most people. In scrap quilts, the number of prints is almost unlimited. Interestingly, the more fabrics you use, the less important any one decision becomes.

More Scraps May Be Better, But Not Required

You may not need as much variety as you think. Look at the 1890s Crib Quilt on page 80. In that quilt, only 40 fabrics were used in the scrap Nine Patch blocks. Also, I use a very liberal definition of scrap fabric. It is any fabric I have in the studio and haven't used. That is, it is all leftover from the last quilt I made, it must be scrap! It doesn't have to be fabric left from cutting out a garment or a quilt.

If, however, for some unimaginable reason you don't have enough 100% cotton fabric scraps to start making scrap Nine Patch blocks, here are some simple solutions.

Let the Word Out

The next time you are in a group of three or more women, just mention that you are looking for fabric scraps. You will be amazed at the bags of fabric that will arrive on your doorstep. Be prepared to sort. If non-quilters start sending bags of fabric, begin immediately to discriminate and eliminate fabrics you feel are completely unsuitable. Don't feel guilty about throwing away or sending some of the fabrics on to another home. The person who gave them to you didn't have the courage and you are doing them a favor!

Everyone has to make his or her own decision about what fabric is acceptable. I'm almost positive I don't want to make a polyester double-knit quilt, but I have a friend who jokes about it. Maybe I would save a small piece before sending it on down the line. I am absolutely positive I wouldn't ever use any bonded acrylics from the late seventies. In my opinion, neither should anyone else! They would be history! Silks, velveteen and wool, however, are fabrics I do enjoy working with, so I would keep some of them, but store them separately.

Buy Creatively

So many quilt shops have fat quarters of fabric available and you can easily acquire variety without having to haul bolts to a cutting table. Look carefully at remnant bins and fabric sales to help you develop a more varied inventory.

At garage sales or thrift stores, look through the racks for prints or plaids you like. It may be a personal idiosyncrasy, but it is difficult for me to cut up my own favorite used clothes, so I save them intact. On the other hand, I have no problem cutting quilt pieces from garments that absolute strangers are throwing away. In fact, I feel just a little noble rescuing those fabrics from certain landfill duty.

Look at department store sale racks on sale days. You know those days when there is another 40% off of already reduced prices! There are some wonderful prints in ready-to-wear that we never see on the bolt. I have been known to find a new garment with a great print and at such a reduced price that I bought it just for the fabric!

Organize a Fabric or Strip Exchange
Or, better yet, see our ideas for a Nine-Patch Swap Meet on page 157. Adapt these ideas as necessary for fabric or pre-cut strip exchanges.

Keeping Scrap Quilts Under Control

Scrap quilts can get out of control and lose their charm. Here are some tips to help prevent ugly scrap quilts. Fortunately the Nine Patch block and many of the quilts have almost built-in safe guards against the uglies!

A common background fabric can help unite a variety of colors. In addition to the 1890s Crib Quilt and the 1890s in Reverse, shown in photographs on pages 80 and 82, many of the illustrations use one background fabric. In some cases you might match one of the fabrics in the Nine Patch blocks with the background fabric and the other fabrics in the Nine Patches would be scrap.

Pick a multicolor print fabric for the border and then only use fabrics that don't look ugly with that print in the Nine Patch blocks. It is important to note you aren't selecting fabrics that look pretty, they just don't look ugly!

Repetition of an accent color can be very calming or controlling to a scrap quilt. In the classic 5/4 Nine Patch block, either position could be used for the consistent accent color or make a 4/4/1 and put the accent in the center of each Nine Patch.

A limited palette can be very effective in calming a scrap quilt. If all of the Nine Patch blocks feature jewel tones or earth tones there is nothing jarring to the eye, but there is still enough variety to create interest. In an even more controlled scrap quilt, every Nine Patch is blue and yellow, but a different blue and yellow. Frankly, this barely qualifies as a scrap quilt to me.

Likewise, a limited range of values puts a degree of control into a scrap quilt. If you put all of your fabrics in order from lightest to darkest, okay, not all of your fabrics, but why not pick a range of forty fabrics and try this? Put your forty fabrics in order from lightest to darkest. Now drop out the 10 lightest or darkest. The remaining fabrics have a more limited range of values and a quilt made with them will reflect that limitation.

Organize a Nine Patch Swap Meet

Nearly everyone has participated in a cookie exchange during the holidays. The concept is simple. Instead of making six different cookie recipes to get the variety of cookies you would like to have, six people are organized to make six dozen cookies each and exchange with each other. The idea is the same for Nine Patch swap meet. The bonus is no calories!

While it is easy to use strips of scraps to create Nine Patch blocks, it is even easier and more efficient to make full-length strips into Nine Patch blocks. So for a quick scrap quilt, organize a group of your friends to make and exchange Nine Patch blocks.

One good way to get a group together is to establish at the beginning that everyone in the group will have a chance to describe the fabric guidelines for the Nine Patch combination. The group can decide if that

opportunity will be by the luck-of-the-draw, by age, reverse alphabetical order, etc?

It is good to establish some guidelines. You want the first attempt to be as successful and fun as possible. That increases the chance that the group will want to continue. There are always different sizes, different color combinations and different styles of Nine Patch blocks for other quilts. The first rule is don't call the guidelines rules!

1. Many proponents of strip techniques say that accuracy in a quarter-inch seam doesn't matter, consistency is all that counts. I used to go along with that, but it doesn't work in a Nine Patch Swap and that fact needs to be emphasized. There are now so many ways to easily get a quarter-inch seam that I believe we should get tough and just do it!

Emphasize the importance of the blocks ending up the same size when you are exchanging. You may photocopy "Test Drive Your Seam Allowance" from this book. Make enough copies for everyone in the group. I would recommend including the three strips of fabric necessary to do the test. It is easier for one person to cut and distribute these test strips than it is to expect everyone to do it independently. The Test Drive also has Nine Patch diagrams you can circle to identify the style to be made.

2. Establish fairly specific guidelines. For example you might describe 1 1/2-inch cut strips, blue and white fabrics, with blue in the 5 position. If what you really want is assorted dark indigo blue fabrics and off-white, that needs to be specified to avoid disappointment. Of course, you must decide whether the fabrics have to be prewashed or not and 100% cotton or not.

If necessary, be specific about what you don't want as well as what you want. If flannel, chartreuse, plaids or juvenile prints are no-no, that should be specified.

3. Establish ahead of time the number of blocks each participant has to complete. As I pointed out in the 1890s Crib Quilt, it is not uncommon for antique scrap quilts to have at least three Nine Patch blocks with the same fabric arrangement. A logical exchange would be three blocks per participant. If there are eight people in the group, everyone would need to make 24 blocks, 12 would need to make 36, etc. For more blocks, you either need more people, or everyone makes and exchanges two combinations.

Remind people that they don't have to have a lot of fabric to participate in a Nine Patch Swap Meet. The real purpose of a Swap is to get variety. Look at the chart on page 14 that tells the number of squares, dependent on size, per fat quarter. Divide the appropriate number by 5 to get the approximate number of 5/4 Nine Patch blocks you can make with two fat quarters of fabric. So, even if they have to make a small purchase, in return they will get the variety of several purchases.

Another fun incentive for the scrap Nine Patch exchange is to do it as part of a challenge quilt program.

The Nine Patch Luncheon

Just in case your friends think you have gone off the deep end with Nine Patch blocks, here is a way to prove it! Pull together a Nine Patch Luncheon.

The centerpiece will be the patchwork arrangement of sandwiches. Pick a large flat tray or even cover a thick piece of Foamcore™ with foil to make a firm flat surface for the sandwich arrangement. As you won't be able to stack any sandwiches, that would spoil the effect, you may want some small extra trays of mini-quilt arrangements. Just as in the book, most of the blocks will be Nine Patch, but you may also want some Fence Rail and half-square triangles. It will depend on how large a tray you plan to fill.

Nine Patch Swap Meet

Test Drive Your Seam Allowance

Test your ¼-inch seam allowance by cutting three 2-inch by 5-inch strips and sewing them together lengthwise. The sewn unit should measure 5 inches square. More importantly, the finished size of the center strip should be a perfect 1½ inches wide. If you don't get these measurements, make an adjustment and repeat the exercise. If your machine needle has an adjustment feature, try moving it one notch at a time until you can sew a perfect ¼-inch seam. Make a note of the machine's setting so you can dial it up any time. If the machine came with a screw-in seam guide accessory, try using it, or make a seam guide by placing a strip of tape on the machine, one-quarter inch from the needle. Also, the local sewing machine dealer may have a special ¼-inch presser foot for your machine.

Arrangement:

5\4 5 Dark   5\4 5 Light   Singleton   or…

Size of cut strips: _____

Block size with seam allowances should be: _____

Color specifications: _____

_____

_____

_____

36 ☐ 48 ☐ 72 ☐ **or**   **blocks due by**

date

Making Patchwork Sandwiches

You can do this several ways, only your imagination and spirit will limit how outrageous this could get! For starters, you need different colors of bread. There is more efficiency and less waste if the slices are generally the same size. When I think of different colors, I think of the variety of white, whole wheat, rye and pumpernickel colors you can find in a store. Some of you are probably already thinking of experimenting by adding food color to the bread you make at home. Some open-faced units here and there could also add a little accent color if needed.

To me, the easiest method is to cut away the crusts, then make the sandwiches and then cut the shapes. However, you could cut the bread into the sizes needed and then make little sandwiches. If you are going to make the sandwiches first, select the fillings with the knowledge that there will be lots of cutting and things that stick to the bread are better than things that fall out at the cut edges.

It is also easier to make the sandwich with one slice of white bread and one of wheat or any second color. With this method, you can just turn a section over to meet the shape requirements and it reduces the chance of height differences. It does mean the bottom of a sandwich section could surprise someone who perhaps dislikes certain breads. Oh well!

Tip — Nine Patch Sandwich

Unless you want to put a complete Nine Patch sandwich on individual plates, don't try to cut a complete Nine Patch out of one sandwich. The pieces are just too small, barely bite size. They are cute, but...Instead, make a sandwich from the most typical trimmed bread size. It should be a square. Cut it into quarters. It will take two and a quarter sandwiches to make a Nine Patch design.

Other Menu Suggestions

• Two different colors of gelatin salads could be cut in squares and rearranged in patchwork formation in a new dish.

• Cheese trays could definitely be arranged in Nine Patch formations.

• Sheet cake from the bakery can easily be frosted in patchwork style or maybe there is a cake decorator in your quilting group that would like to volunteer that effort.

• Neapolitan ice cream sold in rectangular cartons and served by the slice would make nice Fence Rail dessert.

It is definitely a personal decision just how far off the deep-end you are willing to go, but I hope this has started the wheels in motion. Please send letters and pictures and copies of your menu.

What to Do with the Bread Scraps

After you prepare all these sandwiches the quiltmaker attitude will reappear. It will be just like making quilts, you'll have too many scraps to throw away and will look for another project. So, here is a list of suggestions.

1. The easiest way to use the scraps is to feed the birds. Maybe you will be lucky enough to have sunshine, a lake with geese, a grandchild and a bag of bread crusts all on the same day!

2. Dry them to make breadcrumbs.

3. Cube them, then dry and season for croutons.

4. Use them in that recipe you have for Mom's Favorite Bread Pudding.

Mom's Favorite Bread Pudding

2 c. scalded milk
2 T. butter
2 eggs
1/3 c. sugar
1/4 tsp. Salt
1/4 tsp. Nutmeg
1/2 tsp. Vanilla
3-4 c. diced bread
2 T. raisins
2 T. sugar

Cube bread and mix with raisins in a buttered baking dish. Add butter to scalded milk. Beat eggs; add sugar, salt, nutmeg and vanilla. Add to milk and pour over bread and raisins. Mix well and let stand 10 minutes. Sprinkle the 2 T. sugar over the top and bake as custard in pan of hot water until silver knife inserted in center comes out clean.

It seems that bread pudding has become a fashionable dessert in some fine restaurants and I have tasted my share. I can almost guarantee that those fancy versions of bread pudding have substituted cream for at least some of the milk and include more butter, sugar, raisins and nutmeg than Mom's recipe! In addition, they are usually topped with a rich sauce.

Index